Origins:

Native Californians

They made huts of willow and tule, and they were a peaceful tribe, having no weapons nor system of warfare. Many of the Coast Miwok Indians lived on the Point Reyes Peninsula, in Marin County, where they foraged for acorns and berries, scooped clams from the tidal beaches, made garments from elk and deer hides. Today, one hundred and thirteen of their original village sites, some over three thousand years old, have been uncovered, along with reminders of their complex culture—clam disc beads, whalebone wedges, and pestles for grinding grain. The descendants of this ancient tribe are thought to be the "strange" and "naked" people who greeted Northern California's first European visitors in 1579.

The First Europeans

His boat in need of repair, his men near-starved from their diet of water and sea biscuits, Sir Francis Drake careened his ship, the *Golden Hind*, on a sandy beach somewhere in Northern California in 1579. The shores of Drakes Bay, on the Point Reyes Peninsula, are thought by many to be the place where Drake, who had hoped to find a passage to the

Atlantic across the New World, may have landed.

Undaunted by the "thicke mists and most stynk-inge fogges" that shrouded the Pacific Coast, the English explorers found Marin's interior to be a "goodly country, and fruitful soyle, stored with many blessings for the use of man."

The Coast Miwok Indians, believing their bearded white visitors to be dead souls returned to life, presented Drake's crew with gifts—furs, feathers, and baskets of food. On the 23rd of July, 1579, the *Golden Hind* resumed her voyage. The Miwoks, distressed by their visitors' departure, lit ceremonial fires on the ocean cliffs and danced and wailed around them.

Days of the Dons

In 1821, **Mexico won independence** from Spain. Between 1834 and 1846, the Mexican governors of California issued twenty-one land grants in Marin County. Most went to army officers and political favorites. During the "days of the dons," as this period is sometimes called, Hispanic culture prevailed in the county.

When the Mexican government dissolved the Spanish mission system in 1834, the Indian residents of Mission San Rafael Arcangel were left to support themselves. Many were forced to work on the *ranchos,* others died of starvation or succumbed to the white man's diseases. When California joined the Union in 1850, most of the Mexican and Indian claims to the land were disregarded.

Yankee Settlements

With the Gold Rush, many ranchers in Marin prospered, providing San Francisco and the boom towns of the Mother Lode with beef and dairy products. A number of Yankee prospectors who failed to strike it rich settled in Marin, buying ranches or opening businesses similar to those they had owned in the East.

The Yankee settlers left an indelible mark on Marin; their entrepreneurial skills and sober individualism were reflected in their settlements—clapboard shops, houses, schools and churches—a legacy which remains today. Parts of Marin still bear an uncanny resemblance to New England villages and towns.

First the ferries, then the trains, finally the bridges, opened Marin's peaceful hills and valleys to industries and to people eager to build homes in the county. The tension between developers and environmentalists continues today, as construction pierces deeper into the heartland of Marin. Yet, miraculously, one third of the county's land area is public park land.

*For Abigail and Elna*_____

Text copyright © 1981 by Jane Futcher
Color photographs copyright © 1981 by Robert
Conover

Published by Holt, Rinehart and Winston,
383 Madison Avenue, New York,
New York 10017.

Published simultaneously in Canada by Holt,
Rinehart and Winston of Canada, Limited.

Library of Congress Cataloging in Publication
Data

Futcher, Jane
  Marin, the place, the people.

  Includes index.
  1. Marin Co., Calif.—Description and travel.
2. Marin Co., Calif.—History. I. Conover,
Robert. II. Title.
F868.M3F87   979.4′62   80-27986

ISBN: 0-03-057472-2

First Edition
Printed in the United States of America

10 9 8 7 6 5 4 3 2 1

Grateful acknowledgement is made for the use of
the following:

"Calm morning at Drake's Bay" from *The
Morning Glory* by Robert Bly. Copyright © 1974
by Robert Bly. Reprinted by permission of Harper
& Row, Publishers, Inc.

"The Song Mt. Tamalpais Sings," Copyright ©
1973 by Donald Allen for the Estate of Lew Welch.
Reprinted by permission of Grey Fox Press.

"This Place" and "Immigration," Copyright ©
1980 by HOC DOI Project. Reprinted by permission of HOC DOI Project, P.O. Box 5646, San
Francisco, CA 94101.

"this poem is for birds" from *Myths & Texts* by
Gary Snyder. Copyright © 1960 by Gary Snyder.
Reprinted by permission of New Directions.

"Under the second moon" from "The Dragon and
the Unicorn" by Kenneth Rexroth in *Collected
Longer Poems*. Copyright © 1952 by Kenneth
Rexroth. Reprinted by permission of New
Directions.

MARIN

The Place, The People

Profile of a California County

＊

Text by Jane Futcher
Photography and Design by Robert Conover

Holt, Rinehart and Winston • New York

Drakes Estero, Point Reyes National Seashore

Prologue

The sweeping spans of the Golden Gate Bridge reach northward toward Marin County, their orange cables brilliant against the hills beyond. Far below is the mile-wide channel where San Francisco Bay joins the Pacific Ocean. To the east is the widening mouth of the bay, punctuated by an island of rock—Alcatraz, once America's toughest federal prison, now a tourists' mecca; to the west lies the Pacific.

Before us, where the bridge bows and rests, are the rugged cliffs of the Marin Headlands. Three million years of geological upheaval, of folding, faulting, and uplifting created those ridges, which are part of California's Coastal Range mountains. The cliffs drop abruptly into the churning surf of the Golden Gate Channel. *We* descend more slowly, rolling onto the Headlands like a whisperjet arriving in another country. The city is behind us, the chilling fog is gone. The sun breaks through the clouds, casting white light on the stucco homes of Sausalito. Wind flattens the grassy fields of Tiburon, Strawberry Point, and Angel Island. The peaks and sloping ridges of Mount Tamalpais stretch before us. We have entered Marin.

Marin. A triangular peninsula whose western shores are flanked by the Pacific Ocean and whose eastern shores are formed by San Francisco Bay. Her only neighbor is Sonoma County, to the north. Marin. In land area, fourth smallest of California's fifty-eight counties; in population, twenty-sixth smallest; in median income level, number one; in per capita income, number four. Affluent Marin. Beautiful Marin.

Home of Muir Woods and virgin redwoods, of Point Reyes National Seashore, of the Golden Gate National Recreation Area, of Mount Tamalpais and five other state parks. One-third of the county is public parkland, including most of the spectacular Pacific coastline. It is all just a bridge ride from San Francisco, little more than that from Oakland, Berkeley, and the other cities of the East Bay. No major metropolitan area in the world enjoys such a large and dramatically beautiful public space so nearby.

"I live in Marin," someone tells you at a party. You nod; perhaps you even smile. For already you imagine a bubbling hot-tub, a plump portfolio of stocks and bonds, a redwood deck landscaped with red geraniums and marijuana plants. You are speaking, you assume, to an upper-middle-class professional with a job in San Francisco and liberal political leanings. Your Marinite rides a ten-speed on weekends, attends aikido class on Tuesday nights, and puts bean sprouts on Big Macs. If married, has been divorced at least once, and has recently left primal therapy for receptive-listening classes in Mill Valley. If you stick around long enough, you will probably find that on a few counts you have guessed correctly.

There *is* a stereotype of Marin County and its residents; occasionally you meet someone who fits it. But your stereotype will prevail only if you refuse tenaciously to explore the county's coastal hills and rural interior; only if you avoid her tiny fishing villages and friendly, sunlit cafés; only if you never speak to anyone you meet and keep your eyes firmly to the road.

For if you look more closely at Marin, if you walk through the sunken valleys of Point Reyes, talk to an old-timer on the streets of Novato, or stop for a drink at Sausalito's No Name Bar, you will find your stereotype vanishing. You will see that Marin is more than a playground for the rich.

You will find militant political activists as well as dilettantes, newly arrived organic gardeners as well as dairy ranchers whose families have lived in Marin for over one hundred years. You will discover Marin's colorful history: her early days, when the county was proud to be one of the original twenty-seven created by California's first state legislature in 1850. You will hear of the railroads and ferries—in the 1880s and '90s—that opened the county to developers and summer residents from San Francisco, many of whom would settle permanently after the 1906 earthquake and fire. But it was the completion of the Golden Gate Bridge in 1937 that made Marin the accessible bedroom community it is today.

Marin County is a curious mix of affluence and idealism, of isolationism and innovation. Socialites and houseboat artists lie down in front of bulldozers to protest the invasion of Sausalito's waterfront community by profit-seeking developers. Businessmen and Zen Buddhists attend public hearings to discuss the fate of a coastal valley. Single mothers and senior citizens tangle with county supervisors over the need for low-cost housing.

Perhaps that's just affluent California, some say, where people have the time, money, and freedom to get involved in community affairs. But in California there are many affluent counties, and they are not like Marin. Their affluence has brought rigidity and, very often, indifference to social issues. Marin, on the other hand, has more than its share of involved, dynamic citizens willing to fight for causes others eschew. It has been estimated that there are 998 organizations in Marin dedicated to social causes—Mill Valley's Bread and Roses provides free entertainment for prisoners and shut-ins; Sausalito's Commuter Connection has developed a car-pool system to replace solo commuting.

How do we account for the contradictions that seem to abound in Marin? Perhaps the temperament of Marin today is the legacy left by earlier generations: the spirit of cooperation, a blessing left by the peaceful Coast Miwok Indians; today's geniality and love of luxury, the legacy of the Mexican dons who welcomed visitors to their ranches and entertained lavishly. Perhaps the fortune-seekers from freewheeling San Francisco brought to Marin's small towns a liveliness and sophistication most communities lack. And Marin's Swiss-Italian and Portuguese immigrants, who so cherished the county's mild climate? Perhaps they gave their love of the land and the sea and of the burning summer sun. The fierce individualism and ambition? Perhaps these traits came from the Yankee settlers who arrived in the Gold Rush and never left.

And today's settlers? What have they brought? The young people and activists? The singles? The families with children? Perhaps their gift is their mobility, the flexibility that gives them a knack for finding new solutions to problems that seem hopelessly complex.

And perhaps, above all, it is the land itself that makes Marin unique. Poised at the edge of a continent, at the edge of a culture, the Pacific shores, the interior hills and valleys, the bay shores inside the Golden Gate, all have their own character and appeal. The land has welcomed ranchers as well as conservationists, professionals as well as poets, backpacks as well as briefcases.

But, as unique as Marin seems to many of us, in some respects it is typical of every county in America today. Marin too is threatened by the very residents it has welcomed. Developers carve up rural valleys to build houses only the rich can afford. Soaring real-estate prices are driving out the poor, the senior citizens, the artists, who have given Marin its heterogeneous, quirky constitution. Industrial pollution endangers bay marshes, and freshwater streams are dammed for reservoirs.

How Marin will survive the transition to the twenty-first century is of interest to all of America. How the county will deal with the polarities between rich and poor, young and old, profit-makers and conservationists, may be a lesson for all of us. And if there is a land that deserves to survive and a people willing to fight for its future, they can both be found in Marin County.

DERIVATION OF THE NAME MARIN

This county derives its name from Marin, a famous chief of the Lacatuit Indians, who originally occupied this part of California, and who, aided by his people, after having vanquished the Spaniards in several skirmishes that took place between the years of 1815 and 1824, was finally captured by his enemies. Making his escape, Marin took shelter on a little island in the Bay of San Francisco, and which being afterwards called after him, communicated its name to the adjacent mainland. The chief having fallen into the hands of his foes a second time, barely escaped being put to death, through the interference of the priests at the mission San Rafael, who subsequently enjoyed the satisfaction of seeing him converted to the true faith. He died at the mission, which had been the scene of his conversion and rescue, in the year 1834.

ALLEY, BOWEN AND COMPANY
HISTORY OF MARIN COUNTY, CALIFORNIA (1880)

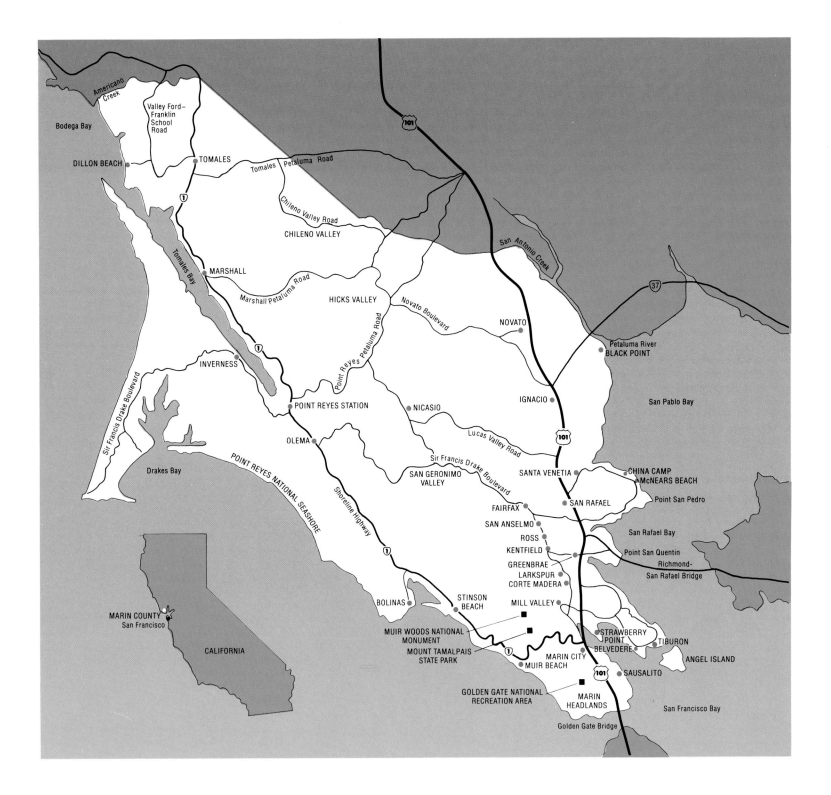

Contents

Part 1

McClures Beach, Point Reyes National Seashore

PACIFIC SHORES: The Western Edge

Chapter 1 ——————— A Land Preserved

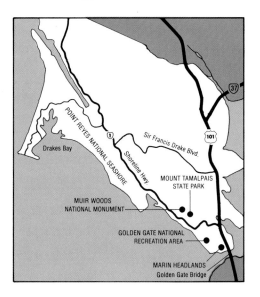

Marin Headlands
Golden Gate National Recreation Area
Mount Tamalpais State Park and
Muir Woods National Monument
Point Reyes National Seashore

Marin Headlands

The red-clay cliffs of the Marin Headlands face the pounding Pacific surf resolutely. Standing at the edge of a continent, they announce to arriving ships the entrance to the Golden Gate; they are the last sight seen by sailors headed for the Orient. They witness the most profound of human events: homecomings and farewells, arrivals and departures, life and death. They protect the bayshores from the attack of the Pacific surf, yet they too are vulnerable, gradually being eroded by the constant pressure of ocean waves.

The Marin Headlands are part of the Golden Gate National Recreation Area and are bordered on the west by the Pacific, on the south by the Golden Gate Channel, on the east by the town of Sausalito. Sausalito today is separated from the Headlands by Highway 101, but in 1838, when Captain William A. Richardson received "Rancho Saucelito," a nineteen-thousand-acre land grant, from the Mexican government, the Headlands merged with the hills of Sausalito in a continuous, cattle-covered range.

Richardson was an affable Englishman whose skill in charting and navigating San Francisco Bay won the respect of the Mexican military. In fact, he later married Maria Martinez, the daughter of the commandant of the Presidio at Yerba Buena, as San Francisco was then called, and with her built an adobe house on the sunny, protected shores of Sausalito. While the Headlands were excellent for grazing cattle, the wind and fog to which they were exposed made them an inhospitable place to build.

California had been part of the Union almost eleven years when the Civil War began in 1861. Although there was no active combat on the West Coast, the United States government was concerned that should another war break out, San Francisco, largest American port on the Pacific, might be

Marin Headlands from San Francisco

4

CAPTAIN RICHARDSON'S DAUGHTER

I, Mrs. Marianna Torres, was born at the Presidio, San Francisco, April 9, 1826. . . . My father, Capt. Richardson, built the first house ever built in San Francisco, in the year 1835. . . . In 1838 my father received a grant of land, consisting of over 19,000 acres of land called the Sausalito Rancho. . . . He brought the first ship in the Golden Gate in 1835, the *Ayacucho,* a trading vessel from Peru, in command of Capt. Wilson. He was also the first pilot. . . .

RECOLLECTIONS OF
MRS. MARIANNA TORRES
1826–1908

GOLDEN GATE NATIONAL RECREATION AREA

There is perhaps no other place on earth where the works of humans and the works of nature meet in such a dramatic and potentially prolific conjunction as at the Golden Gate. It is fitting that fertile seeds of the future be planted on the hills and valleys alongside the historic strait. This is, after all, Chrysopylae, portal to a new age.

HAROLD GILLIAM
EXAMINER-CHRONICLE
CALIFORNIA LIVING MAGAZINE
FEBRUARY 15, 1981

BEFORE THE BRIDGE

I used to look out at the Golden Gate when there was no bridge. We used to take the ferryboat across when Marin had a little bit of isolation that I bet they wish they had again.

DAVID BROWER
JANUARY 16, 1981

vulnerable to enemy attack. In 1866 the army purchased Lime Point, nineteen hundred acres of land in the Headlands, and constructed bunkers and gun emplacements on the high Pacific bluffs. Changing military needs later required the division of Lime Point into three smaller posts: Fort Baker (1897), just east of the Golden Gate Bridge; Fort Barry (1904), adjacent to Point Bonita; and Fort Cronkhite (1937), overlooking the Tennessee Valley.

Ironically, the military presence in the Marin Headlands was more useful in saving the land from domestic invaders—land developers and builders—than from foreign ones. With the completion of the Golden Gate Bridge in 1937, the hills and valleys of southern Marin became far more accessible to commuters from San Francisco. The Headlands, still in the hands of the military, were protected from the surveyor's map and developer's tract houses.

But with World War II and the advent of more sophisticated defense systems, the army's ground installations on the Headlands became obsolete. The slow process of dismantling the forts began. The postwar baby boom sent real-estate prices skyrocketing in Marin; developers eyed the Headlands as a prime site for housing. No story better reveals the county's conflicting interests than that of Marincello.

In 1964 the Frouge Corporation, a Connecticut development company, held a gala party in Sausalito, unveiling the model of a city they proposed to build on the Marin Headlands. The site, which had been purchased by the Gulf Oil Corporation from the U.S. Army, was located on the shores of Rodeo Lagoon. The new town would be called Marincello, "where the mountains meet the sea."

Around the lagoon, where Captain Richardson's cattle had once grazed, the corporation envisioned a city of twenty to twenty-five thousand people, with some twenty high-rise apartment buildings, as well as single-family homes, town houses, and a resort hotel. One thousand acres of the land would house commercial properties, including retail stores and light industry. Impressed with the company's planning concepts, such as "urban decentralization" and "cluster" housing, in November 1965 the Marin County Board of Supervisors reluctantly approved the development.

For almost five years, shock waves from that decision

Golden Gate Bridge under construction, 1933

"BOAT PEOPLE" AT THE GOLDEN GATE

...Two families of "boat people" from Vietnam have begun a puzzling new life in the United States in an improbable setting— a former Army barracks at Fort Cronkhite just north of the Golden Gate.... The refugees are living in a former Nike missile barracks, which is now used as housing by the Yosemite Institute, an ecology school....

SAN FRANCISCO CHRONICLE
JANUARY 26, 1979

Marine Mammal Center, Marin Headlands

vibrated through the county. Many Marinites were alarmed by the prospect of a development that would increase population density and spoil one of Marin's most distinctive natural landmarks. Traffic alone, it was said, would require the construction of a second bridge across the Golden Gate or the addition of a new span above the old bridge.

Even as the access road to the site neared completion, citizens' groups fought Marincello. In the courts, in public hearings, and in the press, conservationists decried the environmental, traffic, and density hazards Marincello would introduce. In January 1969, just a few months before Marincello was, in effect, dealt a death blow by the California Supreme Court, Thomas Frouge, "father" of Marincello, died of a massive cerebral hemorrhage. Although his heirs continued to fight for Marincello, a series of financial and legal woes caused Gulf Oil, the project's sponsor, to withdraw its backing. In November 1970, Marincello breathed its last gasp.

Golden Gate National Recreation Area

Concerned that other developers might someday succeed in building on the Headlands, a coalition of conservationists called People for a Golden Gate National Recreation Area was formed in 1971 to pressure the federal government to purchase the Headlands for a public park. And in October 1972 it came to pass. President Richard M. Nixon signed into law a bill creating the Golden Gate National Recreation Area, of which the Headlands would be a part.

Today the GGNRA includes some thirty-four thousand acres of land, stretching from Fort Funston, on San Francisco's Pacific coast, north across the Golden Gate, through the Headlands, Muir Beach, Muir Woods National Monument, and the Point Reyes National Seashore. Many mothballed army barracks in the recreation area now house nonprofit Bay Area organizations. Thus, at Fort Barry, one barracks is a youth hostel; at Fort Baker, army residences may be converted to low-cost housing for artists; and at Fort Cronkhite, a former Nike missile site is the home of the California Marine Mammal Center, which rehabilitates injured or abandoned marine mammals and returns them to the ocean.

It is an eerie feeling to walk through the Headlands and see the curious mixture of unconventional citizens' groups alongside decaying gun emplacements, bunkers, and barracks. It is as if the pacifists of the 1960s had placed not just a single daisy into the rifle barrel of a National Guardsman, but an entire field of flowers. Two faces of the American dream cry out across the bare hills and valleys of southern Marin.

Mount Tamalpais State Park and Muir Woods National Monument

Mount Tamalpais, Marin's only true mountain, presides benignly over the county, her three peaks, each almost half a mile high, forming a majestic silhouette that can be seen from Sonoma, Napa, Contra Costa, Solano, and San Francisco counties. Easily Marin's most dramatic visual landmark, the mountain dominates the county. Many Marinites say that the mountain brought them to the county. She called them, beckoned, demanded they climb her ridges, live in her valleys, respect her power.

Mount Tamalpais is thought to have derived its name from a Coast Miwok Indian tribe, sometimes called the Tamals, who lived in the mountain's bayshore valleys. *Pais* was the Tamal word for mound or mountain; Tamalpais meant "bay mountain," or mountain of the Tamals. Steep canyons and dense chaparral made the upper slopes of Tamalpais inaccessible to the Tamals and to nineteenth-century settlers. But in the early 1900s, even Redwood Canyon, a steep ravine on the western slopes, was threatened by a private water company, which planned to cut the redwoods, dam Redwood Creek, and sink the canyon beneath a reservoir.

William Kent, a Marin resident and later a U.S. congressman, was alarmed by this threat to the last virgin redwoods of Tamalpais and by the possibility of future residential development of the mountain. In 1908 he purchased the land and deeded it to the U.S. government, persuading President Theodore Roosevelt to establish a national monument in Redwood Canyon. The land was called Muir Woods, after John Muir, Kent's friend, a conservationist who had worked unflaggingly to preserve California's wilderness.

At least one private enterprise benefited from the establishment of a national park at Muir Woods: the Tamalpais Scenic Railway. That company was already attracting thousands of tourists each week with "the crookedest railroad in the

**The Mountain Theater
Mount Tamalpais State Park**

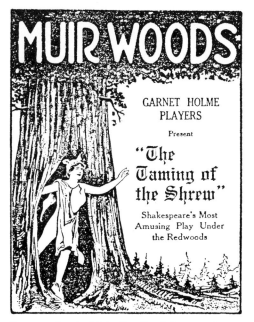

MUIR WOODS

GARNET HOLME
PLAYERS

Present

"The
Taming of
the Shrew"

Shakespeare's Most
Amusing Play Under
the Redwoods

Program for the Muir Woodland theatre, 1915

RUNNING ON THE MOUNTAIN

On late summer days during the middle of the week, the trails of Tam are little traveled. Even the wild creatures are hidden away somewhere, avoiding the heat. On such days you can sometimes see an ambitious runner laboring up the Grade from the bottom, then coasting down again. But today I'm not that ambitious. Having bummed a ride to a point near the top, I'm running downhill all the way, enjoying the hypnotic rhythm of my feet on the hard surface, playing energy games with gravity as I descend, thankful for the superb view as the Grade swings outward to the edge of the mountain, thankful for the shade as it curves in to cross a mountain stream.

GEORGE LEONARD
THE ULTIMATE ATHLETE (1964)

WOMAN SLAIN ON TAMALPAIS

A 26-year-old woman was found shot to death near a Mount Tamalpais hiking trail yesterday in the same general area where two other women were murdered within the past 14 months. . . .

INDEPENDENT JOURNAL
OCTOBER 16, 1980

world," an eight-mile, narrow-gauge train running from Mill Valley to the East Peak of Tamalpais. A new leg was added: a gravity tram car from Tam's West Peak to Muir Woods. Tourists packed both the rides and delighted in the unique panoramas of the Pacific Ocean and San Francisco Bay.

In 1929 the Tamalpais Railway was destroyed by fire. But the mountain itself was on its way to becoming a state park, proposed by the Tamalpais Conservation Club. The original Mount Tamalpais State Park covered only 892 acres. Today the park includes 6,205 acres. Its northeastern slopes are adjoined by the Mount Tamalpais Watershed—18,570 acres of land, including five reservoirs and many miles of hiking trails administered by the Marin Municipal Water District. Mount Tamalpais State Park is also carved with well-maintained trails that run through a varied jumble of rock formations common in Marin: limestone, metamorphic rock, and intermittent hunks of serpentine. This strange geological mix was created by the seismic activity along the San Andreas Fault, where the North American crustal plate grinds laterally against the Pacific plate. The fault crosses Marin diagonally, slicing through the county from Tomales Bay to Bolinas, where it runs to sea. The fault, and the ever-present threat of earthquake activity, provide Marin residents with an interesting geological as well as psychological environment. The possibility of an earthquake, with its epicenter directly beneath the county, underscores the sense of living on the edge of the continent, as well as the edge of security.

Point Reyes National Seashore

You stand at twilight on a high rib of land that rises from the Point Reyes Peninsula like the spine of a sleeping beast. To the north, the land slips and sinks into Drakes Estero, then rises again where the two-pronged claw of the peninsula curls twelve miles into the Pacific. Is it straining to reach the low-slung tanker cruising just beyond its grasp? Or is it trying to touch the rugged Farallon Islands, granite specks on the horizon, which may once have been part of the same land mass? The underside of the menacing point forms the white-cliffed rim of a sweeping bay—Drakes Bay. Many historians believe that Sir Francis Drake and the crew of the battered *Golden Hind* may have sailed across these waters before

WAS IT DRAKES BAY?

...it pleased God to send us into a fair and good baye with a good wind to enter same. In this baye wee ankered the seventeenth of June.

RICHARD HAKLUYT
THE FAMOUS VOYAGE OF
SIR FRANCIS DRAKE (1598)

OZONE HIGH

For pure, unadulterated sea air, full of fog and oxygen, charged with ozone, salubrious and salsuginous, invigorating and life-giving air, that will make the pulses leap and bring the roses to the cheek, one should go to Point Reyes, where it can be had at first hand, bereft of nothing.

ALLEY, BOWEN AND COMPANY
HISTORY OF MARIN COUNTY, CALIFORNIA (1880)

Thistle, Point Reyes National Seashore

careening their ship in Drakes Estero.

Here on Inverness Ridge, wind shivers through the needles of the bishop pines; turkey vultures and sparrow hawks spiral above the chaparral. The descending sun transforms the pale stratus clouds into the pink and white layers of a Napoleon pastry. A harder, reflective light flares off the icy surface of the sea. The air is cooler now, the light fading. The green pines are black shapes moving eerily in the wind. In the brush behind you, a sparrow or a rabbit rustles unexpectedly. The lone howl of a dog seems to announce to the natural world that their hour has come. Point Reyes belongs to the animals now, to the earth, to the ocean, perhaps even to the spirits, to He'Koo Las, the Miwok sun goddess, and O'-ye, the Coyote Man.

You tremble as the cold fingers of darkness wrap around you. This magical peninsula, only thirty miles from a huge conglomerate of towns and cities, is one of the last coastal areas in America that has not been gouged and cemented into uneasy silence.

The Solemn Land is the title Marin historian Jack Mason chose for his book on the Point Reyes Peninsula. It is a name appropriate for these isolated hills and valleys, for a place perched on the edge of the continent and separated from the rest of Marin by a rumbling, growling, mile-wide rift in the earth known as the San Andreas Fault, running diagonally beneath the county. Although the damage caused by the earthquake of 1906 was far greater in San Francisco, the movement of the earth was more dramatic here, where the entire peninsula lurched from sixteen to twenty feet northwestward. And it is *still* moving—between one-half and two inches a year—as the Pacific plate, of which Point Reyes is a part, grinds laterally against the North American plate, which runs under mainland Marin. Geologists speculate that Point Reyes was once an island, which in the last eighty million years may have traveled three hundred miles northward, after breaking off from the Tehachapi Mountains in Southern California. Not surprisingly, this unusual geological activity has had a curious effect on the landscape of Point Reyes. "Along the entire zone," writes Harold Gilliam in *An Island in Time*, "are humped-up ridges, ponds with no outlets, odd escarpments, streams running in illogical directions, and a general jumble of

Poppies and lupine
Point Reyes National Seashore

FLORA AND FAUNA

Although Point Reyes comprises less than one-tenth of one percent of California's land area, the Park Service estimates that over fifteen percent of California's plant life— some 750 species—can be found here. Bird watchers for the Point Reyes Observatory have counted 338 species of birds, including several species of pelicans, egrets, herons, and hawks. Point Reyes is the only place on the American continent where the common murre, an auk with coloring not unlike the penguin, will breed. Thirty-seven species of land mammals, including mountain lions and land beavers, are still found on Point Reyes, as well as a number of marine mammal species, including sea lions, harbor seals, and occasionally, the elephant seal. Tule elk, which once inhabited most of Marin County, are now being reintroduced by the National Park Service.

earth features of many different ages where the surface has been fractured or crumpled over periods of hundreds and perhaps thousands of years."

Very little was known about Point Reyes' complex geology in 1836, when Irishman James Berry and Mexican corporal Rafael Garcia were repaid for their services to the Mexican government with land grants on the Point Reyes Peninsula. What both men *did* know was that the peninsula's rolling hills and valleys, kept green almost year-round by coastal fog, were ideal for grazing longhorn cattle.

Two ambitious Yankee lawyers from Vermont, Oscar and James Shafter, capitalized on boundary disputes after the Mexican-American War. They were perhaps the only men in the county familiar with the subtleties of property law. By 1870 they had received, in lieu of fees, almost the entire peninsula, which they subdivided and leased as dairy ranches. English milking cows replaced longhorn cattle, and the dairy industry thrived on Point Reyes.

"The produce of Point Reyes," announced the 1880 *History of Marin County*, "can be summed up in one word—butter. The one great and all-absorbing industry is dairying, and in fact there is no other industry in the township. . . . There is no more extensive dairy in the township than that owned by A. J. Pierce on Tomales Point, and none are better conducted. . . ." The Pierce Ranch operated continuously until the late 1970s, when the ranch was acquired by the Department of Interior for the National Seashore. Several other dairies still operate today, leasing back their ranchland from the National Park Service. Local ranchers whose families have worked the land for many decades have mixed feelings about the government's presence at Point Reyes. While recognizing the benefits of public parks, many ranchers resent being forced to give up their land; and few can afford to buy dairies elsewhere.

Today, almost two million visitors a year come to enjoy Point Reyes National Seashore—to hike the 110 miles of trails that wind along Inverness Ridge and the ocean valleys, to explore the long, windswept beaches of Limantour Spit, Drakes Bay, Kehoe, Sculptured Beach, and McClures. By far the most popular attraction is the Point Reyes Lighthouse, built in 1870 on the promontory of the Point Reyes Headlands. In the past four centuries, more than fifty ships have been wrecked along the peninsula. One can only imagine how many more shipwrecks the lighthouse and foghorn have prevented. One of the coldest places in continental America in the summer months—when the temperature averages about fifty-four degrees Fahrenheit—Point Reyes is only four degrees cooler in winter, when the gray whales migrating from the Bering Sea to Baja California can be seen from its ledges.

Point Reyes Lighthouse

Tide pool, Point Reyes National Seashore

CALM MORNING AT DRAKES BAY

A sort of roll develops out of the bay, & lays itself all down this long beach . . . the hiss of the water wall two inches high, coming in, steady as lions, or African grass fires. Two gulls with feet the color of a pumpkin walk together on the sand. A snipe settles down . . . three squawks . . . the gulls agree to chase it away. Then the wave goes out, the waters mingle so beautifully, it is the mingling after death, the silence, the sweep—so swift!—over darkening sand . . . the airplane sweeping low over the African field at night, lost, no tin cans burning, the old woman stomps around her house on a cane, no lamp lit yet . . .

ROBERT BLY
From POINT REYES POEMS (1974)

The Golden Gate from the Marin Headlands

Marin Headlands

Point Bonita Light

. . . from Highway 101, San Rafael

. . . from the Berkeley Hills

. . . from the Larkspur Ferry

. . . from Corte Madera Creek

. . . from Gate 5, Sausalito

MOUNT TAMALPAIS

. . . from Highway 37, Solano County

Cataract Falls

Mount Tamalpais
Watershed

Tamalpais ridges from Panoramic Highway

Alpine Lake

MUIR WOODS

California buckeye

Miner's lettuce

Coast redwoods

Sword fern

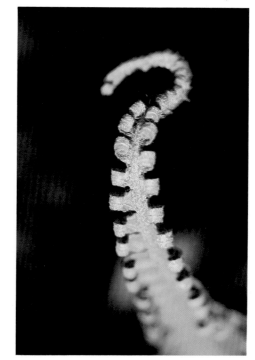

Pasture land

POINT REYES
NATIONAL SEASHORE

Point Reyes Beach

Pierce Point Ranch, Point Reyes National Seashore

Dairy ranch, Drakes Estero

Oyster farm, Drakes Estero

Tule elk herd, Point Reyes National Seashore

McClures Beach, Point Reyes National Seashore

Sculptured Beach, Point Reyes National Seashore

Chapter 2 —————— Beside the Boundaries

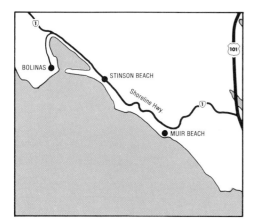

Muir Beach
Stinson Beach
Bolinas

Muir Beach

Muir Beach is a thumbnail-shaped slit in the Pacific Coast. It is the first beach on the Shoreline Highway, and its charm lies in its smallness. The beach itself is part of the Golden Gate National Recreation Area, but the bluff on the north side of the cove is privately owned. Since the 1920s, summer cottages, packed closely together on the precipice, have gazed down on the blue water, where Wendy, the golden retriever cared for by the community, now crawls into the foam to retrieve a stick cast by a bather.

"Muir Beach was awful in the 1950s," says Constance Richardson, her eyes following a wave of smoke rising from her cigarette into the skylight of a Mill Valley restaurant. Richardson, a filmmaker, grew up at Green Gulch Ranch, which slices down the southwestern side of Mount Tamalpais to Muir Beach.

"There was this sleazy bar called Doc O'Brian's," she continues. "They had pinball machines and a jukebox. Pilots from Hamilton Air Force Base used to hang out there on weekends."

Constance's stepfather, George Wheelwright, a physicist and inventor who co-invented Polaroid at the Land-Wheelwright labs in Boston, bought Green Gulch Ranch from a horse rancher in 1945. The story of the family's life in Marin unfolds like a romantic novel. "My mother, Hope Livermore, was a raging society beauty," says Constance. "She knew Scott Fitzgerald and all the beautiful people in Paris. Always being written about. Her picture was on the cover of *Vogue*." Constance sighs; it wasn't easy being the only daughter of a *femme fatale.*

When Constance's father died and her mother married George, the newlyweds decided to leave stodgy life in the East and start again in California. They were driving along

Sea stacks, Shoreline Highway

Heather field, Muir Beach

THIS POEM IS FOR BIRDS
A hawk drifts into the far sky.
A marmot whistles across huge rocks.
Rain on the California hills.
Mussels clamp to sea-boulders
Sucking the Spring tides

Rain soaks the tan stubble
Fields full of ducks

Rain sweeps the Eucalyptus
Strange pines on the coast . . .

GARY SNYDER
From MYTHS & TEXTS (1960)

Shoreline Highway on their honeymoon, when George spotted Green Gulch Ranch and without a second's hesitation, decided to buy it.

"It was a child's dream come true," says Constance. "After dancing class and proper private schools in Connecticut, living on a ranch was a joy. Of course, in the beginning, George didn't have all the kinks worked out." She laughs. "Sometimes salamanders popped out of the faucets, and peacocks screeched around the property like a pack of madwomen."

But George Wheelwright took up the study of farming with the same fervor and dedication with which he had studied physics at Harvard. He introduced a special breed of Australian grass requiring so little water it stayed green all summer, allowing cattle to graze on the upper fields. In the valley he installed lightweight aluminum irrigation pipes. Most of the local ranchers at that time were well-seasoned Portuguese, who viewed Wheelwright skeptically.

"They snickered about George and his Harris tweed jackets until they saw that he was getting higher yields than they were." When Wheelwright bought a prizewinning Hereford in England and flew it to San Francisco, local columnist Herb Caen referred to the Green Gulch residents as "millionaires with hot and cold running udders."

But the affluent times seemed slow in coming. Constance remembers occasions when her mother's society friends would drop in from the East. She grins. "The house was usually a mess. Suddenly the prince and princess of God-knows-where would arrive. Mother would scrounge up some champagne and paté and a white linen tablecloth. We'd picnic outside and my brothers and stepbrothers and I pretended we always lived that way." While Constance's mother entertained the guests with stories about the ranch—"our little experiment"—George would pace uncomfortably, eager to get back to work.

After his wife's death in 1967, Wheelwright sold Green Gulch to the San Francisco Zen Center, which converted the ranch into a farm and retreat for its members. Today the weathered milking barn is the spiritual center for the Zen Buddhists. The old hayloft is the Zendo, or meditation room, and the horse stalls next to the milking troughs are private offices. Extensive vegetable gardens, lovingly cultivated by

JOURNEY TO THE EDGE OF THE WORLD

By virtue of its hilly landscape, its redwood forests and eucalyptus groves, its wayward coastline, and its liberally bohemianized population, the peninsula of Southern Marin has attracted imaginative people from all over the world. Unless I am mistaken or bewitched, I would judge that during the past twenty years it has also become a powerful spiritual center of the nation ... as befits the fact that its geographical center is a mountain holy to the Indians, and named after their princess Tamalpa.

ALAN WATTS
IN MY OWN WAY (1972)

Restaurant, Stinson Beach

Green Gulch residents, provide fare for the Zen Center's restaurant, Greens, in San Francisco.

Recently, Constance Richardson moved back to Marin after raising her kids in Boston. She finds the county very different from the days of her childhood. "I guess you can never go home again," she says wistfully. "I couldn't afford to buy a house in Marin. In 1979 the average home sold for $149,000. I almost moved to Daly City. At the last minute the broker found two little cabins on Panoramic, right on Mount Tamalpais, just a few miles from Muir Beach. It was perfect. Barbara Schwartz, a gentle twenty-three-year-old woman who owned her own bread-baking business, was the tenant. Just after the deal closed, I learned that Barbara had been stabbed to death on a Sunday afternoon walking with her dog on the mountain. I know the house has nothing to do with the murder," Constance whispers. "But how awful. I'm really frightened now. I love to run on the mountain; I wanted my children to." She pauses. "I guess," she says slowly, "there are no safe places anymore ... anywhere."

Stinson Beach

The wind sweeps across Stinson Beach, whipping the sand into funnel-shaped swirls, fanning through the pages of a book propped on the stomach of a sunbather. A ranger walks deliberately toward a woman whose three dogs gallop leashless along the water's edge. At the locked-gate community of Seadrift, on the Stinson sandspit, three surf-casters stand knee-deep in the waves; in their chest-high rubber waders, they are farmers of the sea.

Four motorcycles are parked in front of Ed's Superette in the village of Stinson. The bikes match up with four pairs of legs dangling over the front steps of the market. A beer can pops open, and the men laugh as a teenage girl leaps out of a purple Pinto, her flip-flops scuffing against the cement.

Across the road, a backpacker and a jogger wait for the Golden Gate bus to take them back over the mountain. Near them, at the intersection of Highway 1 and the beach road, two young boys, red-faced with anger, yell insults at each other, circling like sharks the wire garbage bin between them. The long line of cars on the highway moves still more slowly as drivers crane to see the boys, now wrestling in the

RUNNING THE DIPSEA

I put on my Nike Elites, my blue Dolphin shorts, my yellow marathon T-shirt. I would run the Dipsea trail to Stinson Beach; the Dipsea, which every runner knows is the hardest trail in the whole world. Although it is only 7.1 miles, it goes from sea level to sea level and there is a mountain in between.

It starts with 671 steps that are etched into the side of the first ridge. . . . The route reads like Pilgrim's Progress: Dynamite Hill, Cardiac Hill, Insulin Hill, Slough of Despond. All the hills are straight up, and uniquely, they don't have a down side to them. But it is Hog's Back Rise, the least steep, that takes the heart out of you because it is so long and pitiless. . . .

But oh! Oh boy! If you can get up Cardiac and you have any energy left at all, then, oh then will come the run of your life. . . .

And you run, how you run, down to the glittering sea, a seeming sub-four-minute-mile pace.

SUSAN TROTT
WHEN YOUR LOVER LEAVES YOU (1980)

BY THE BEAUTIFUL SEA

"So exhilarating are the air and water that ladies crossing the beach are seen to flip a handspring."

Quoted by JACK MASON
LAST STAGE FOR BOLINAS (1973)

dirt. One of the cyclists strides across the street and pulls the boys apart. They stop, then race down the road, past the post office, where two blond surfers whisk a Frisbee over the roofs of parked cars. An impatient motorist leans on his horn, cueing the trail of cars behind him. Drinks in hand, guests at the Sand Dollar Restaurant stand on the front porch to check out the noise; a broker for Shoreline Realty next door, and the manager of the bookstore across the street, walk down to the intersection. The blue, winking light of a state trooper car appears from nowhere. Cops get out and wave the gawkers on. In five more minutes it's just another Sunday at Stinson Beach.

There's never been a lack of summertime activity at Stinson. In the 1880s, when the place was known as Easkoot's Beach, weekend and summer visitors flocked to the long stretch of white sand at the western foot of Mount Tamalpais. Captain Alfred Easkoot was not always a friendly host. According to local stories, he guarded the beach with a shotgun and fired a warning shot at any beachcomber who picked up driftwood. When lawyer Archie Upton converted the beach into a tent city for vacationers, life mellowed. But Upton, who inherited Willow Camp from his stepfather, Nathan Stinson, had his troubles too.

Some of them were caused by William Kent, who was eyeing the property at Stinson with a mind to building a railroad from Steep Ravine on Tamalpais down to Stinson Beach, then north along the sandspit and across the channel to Bolinas. Kent purchased the ravine and a large portion of the sandspit, constructing the Dipsea Inn at Stinson, which he called "a miniature Sahara." The railroad was delayed by legal tangles over land ownership, and the project was abandoned in 1906, when the great earthquake crumbled old houses and new dreams in its wake. Fifty years later the Kent property on the sandspit was surveyed and parceled into one of the most exclusive locked-gate communities on the California coast—Seadrift. Today the spit is almost as inaccessible as the beach itself was when Easkoot clutched his shotgun; residents can only enter by passing a plastic card through a computerized slot, and visitors need special permission. But Stinson Beach continues to be the most popular and well-used beach in the San Francisco Bay Area.

Fishing buoys, Bolinas

THE WRECK OF THE S. S. LEWIS

Through the grey murk, a mere shadow of a large ship became discernible, and in the calm water behind the rocky reef, lifeboats from the stranded vessel were already approaching shore. . . .

When Don Gregorio noted the size of the wrecked craft, he immediately began preparations for his unexpected guests. From the hacienda, cartloads of kettles were brought. Cauldrons (only a few years ago they had been used for "tyring" out the fat of slaughtered cattle) of soup were started, containing sizeable chunks of beef and vegetables from the Briones garden. Indian women made mounds of tortillas (the nourishing corn cakes which are the base of Mexican meals) and from the exposed rocks of the reef, bags of mussels were gathered and steamed in kelp on the edges of the bonfires . . . .

MARIN PEPPER
A NARRATIVE OF THE DAYS OF THE DONS (1965)

Bolinas

For a heron, Bolinas is a twelve-mile flight due north from San Francisco. If your wings are rusty, you can drive most of the way on the Shoreline Highway, which curls north along the Pacific bluffs like a cat's claws. Stalwarts might prefer to sail, as the first Mexican settlers did in the 1830s. The five-hour schooner voyage from San Francisco was not very popular even then. But navigating the heavy seas and the treacherous entry into Bolinas Lagoon past Duxbury Reef was still easier than riding the Miwok trails over the ridges of Tamalpais.

In 1834 the Mexican government granted Rafael Garcia a nine-thousand-acre tract called Rancho Baulenes. His land was in the vicinity of present-day Bolinas. Garcia moved his family and cattle north to the Olema Valley in 1837, leaving Rancho Baulenes in the hands of his brother-in-law, Gregorio Briones.

Describing the life of these early California ranchers, H. H. Bancroft wrote in 1888: "Opening their eyes in the morning, they saw the sun. They breathed fresh air, and listened to the sound of birds; mounting their steeds, they rode forth in the enjoyment of healthful exercise; they tended their flocks, held intercourse with each other, and ran up a fair credit with heaven. . . . "

When Gregorio Briones leased logging rights on Bolinas Ridge to Yankee lumbermen in 1849, he was ill prepared for the tough, hard-drinking laborers who provided Gold Rush San Francisco with timber. The lumbermen called Briones and his family "greasers," and in little more than a decade they stripped Bolinas Ridge of redwoods. "Jugtown," on Bolinas Lagoon, had a saloon—the Gavitt Hotel—where Yankees slugged down their whiskey. Sawmills and shacks and more saloons sprang up at Dogtown, three miles north of Bolinas. In 1850, when the total population of Marin County was 352, 200 of those people were in Bolinas.

The lagoon, where schooners loaded cargoes of lumber and cattle, was slowly silting up with runoff from the mills. Ships could no longer tie up at Bolinas wharf. Flat barges carried cargoes to boats in deeper water.

The Christian temperance movement gained a firm foothold in the town in the 1860s, and the call for sobriety was

DUXBURY REEF

We start walking west. The tide draws back to let us pass, and the farther we go, the quieter and more subdued we feel, as nature grows larger and civilization drops back behind us. There are cliffs made out of earth and rock to our right, cliffs so organic they look like the beginning of the world. Strange pebbles with holes in them are under our feet; the gulls circle timelessly. We approach a vast silence.

CHARLES REICH
THE SORCERER OF BOLINAS REEF (1976)

IN THIS TOWN

In this town people seem to get together with greater ease. Numerous meetings take place in the street, at the post office, in the laundromat, the Store, the Bar, Scowley's, Tarantino's restaurant, on the beach. There are a great number of town events and festivals at which everyone is welcome, such as poetry readings, concerts, film showings, exhibits, potluck dinners, dances and happenings. One goes if one wants, or stays home if one wants. Such public gatherings create little sense of anyone's being "in" or "out." They engender little social competition. There is no jockeying for invitations to the houses of the select. It is perfectly acceptable for a woman or a man to be alone. The fear of being left out or lonely is diminished. There is a certain democracy of social life, and although I cannot prove it, I know it continues to flourish because we have not allowed ourselves to grow too large.

ORVILLE SCHELL
THE TOWN THAT FOUGHT TO SAVE ITSELF (1976)

heard from the hall of the Druid Society, and from the Presbyterian, Methodist, and Catholic churches. A new kind of resident began to appear in the empty houses where lumbermen once lived—artists and summer visitors. Traveling to the village was easier now: on the ocean road twisting along the Pacific bluffs from Sausalito, and on the Scenic Railway, which, after 1896, ran from Mill Valley to the East Peak of Mount Tamalpais. At the West Point Inn, passengers bound for Bolinas boarded a stage.

A stormy night in January 1971. Wind whips the ocean into swelling heads of white foam. Just outside the Golden Gate, two tankers collide in the darkness. Thousands of gallons of oil pour into the water and wash up on the Marin shores. Seabirds, wings flattened in the sticky goo, lie helpless on Stinson and Bolinas beaches. The delicate ecology of the lagoon, and the tidepools on Duxbury Reef, are endangered by this blanket of oil. The people of Bolinas are shocked. With conservationists and naturalists from all parts of the county, they walk the beaches, erect sea screens to prevent more oil from washing into the lagoon, rescue the injured birds and harbor seals. A few are saved; most die.

The event unites Bolinas. Poets, professionals, and weekend visitors work side by side, brought together by a crisis they did not cause, whose effects they must live with. They realize that there is power in working together, and that if they are to keep their own community intact, as they want it, they can and must use this power.

Another crisis may be facing them. The county is planning to build a new sewer system for Bolinas and Stinson Beach. With the capacity to serve some twenty thousand people, it may open up the sparsely populated hills and valleys of Bolinas to subdivision. To improve access, the county has proposed straightening and widening Shoreline Highway.

The people take action, recalling the old board and electing five new members to the Bolinas Public Utilities District (B-PUD), which is the primary governing body in the unincorporated community. A committee is formed to create a plan for Bolinas that will guide future land use, zoning, and environmental protection. It contains the residents' vision of Bolinas as they would like it to be—self-sufficient, small,

Trail sign, Audubon Canyon Ranch, Bolinas

GHOST SHRIMP OF BOLINAS LAGOON

The California Fish and Game Commission voted unanimously yesterday to halt the use of hydraulic process for taking ghost shrimp in Marin County's Bolinas Lagoon. . . .

Marin County supervisors, the Audubon Canyon Ranch and several conservation groups asked for the moratorium because of concern that the hydraulic operations could have a devastating effect on the lagoon's ecosystem.

The shiny, white shrimp, prized as bait for catching sturgeon and striped bass, also is an important food for egrets, great blue herons and other marine birds. The Audubon Canyon Ranch, adjacent to Bolinas Lagoon, is a major nesting place for egrets and herons.

SAN FRANCISCO CHRONICLE
MARCH 31, 1979

dedicated to alternative forms of energy, agriculture, waste disposal, and housing.

In 1975 the Bolinas community plan is accepted. The sewer project has already been defeated.

Other visions are realized. Local school board reps from Bolinas persuade the school district to open an alternative elementary school. A town paper—*The Hearsay News*—is started. A radio station run by volunteers broadcasts community news and programming from the attic of the B-PUD. An adult-education school, The Faultline Institute, is begun at the old Druid Hall outside the town. Bolinas is a community and will continue to be a community. That is how the people want it.

1927. Arthur and Ruth Smadbeck purchased three hundred acres of land on the Bolinas Mesa and mapped out over five thousand tiny lots on its windblown bluffs. An advertisement appeared in the *San Francisco Bulletin*, offering a lot in Bolinas to any new subscriber:

$69.50 Payable!
$9.50 Down! $3.50 a month!
Subscribe for only six months to the
San Francisco Bulletin!!!

Although the *Bulletin* soon abandoned the scheme, the Smadbecks continued to sell their twenty-by-one-hundred-foot lots for many years. A number of buyers did not build their houses until they retired in the mid-1960s, when other new residents were also arriving—college graduates, dropouts from Haight-Ashbury, young people searching for a new life and a place where they could live close to the land, *on* the land. The Smadbeck retirees were not happy to find their paradise swarming with hippies, poets, and idealistic newcomers.

Adrianne White (a pseudonym) *was* happy, watching builders hammer the last nails into her home in Bolinas in 1968. A retired librarian, she had moved to Bolinas to watch birds. She loved birds. All kinds of birds. She knew she would find them—at the Point Reyes Bird Observatory, three miles north of town, and at the Audubon Canyon Ranch, on Bolinas La-

"Who is there to visit in New York anyway? Everybody's moved to Bolinas. . . ."

PHILIP WHALEN
Quoted in ON THE MESA (1971)

SAROYAN ON WELCH

And he [Lew Welch] drove to Gary Snyder's little cabin on the outskirts of Mill Valley, where horses grazed in a field, and Gary, returned from Japan, continued his study of Zen Buddhism. He walked in and there was his friend, and Joanne Kyger, the beautiful young poetess from Vallejo who had the battiest ways. And Lew hung up his ring— his wedding ring—up on a nail on the wall of Gary's cabin, and said, "Mary and me have split, and from now on I'm just a cabdriver and poet and I need a glass of wine."

It was summertime. Everybody laughed.

ARAM SAROYAN
GENESIS ANGELS: THE SAGA OF LEW WELCH AND THE BEAT GENERATION (1979)

ON THE MESA

On the main road of the mesa, a 1964 Chevelle Malibu station wagon pulled over. "Wanna ride?" called the driver.

"O.K.," I said, and got in. The driver was one of our town's innumerable Burn Outs. Most are in their twenties and look like either Charlie Manson or Janis Joplin. This Burn Out was wearing horn-rimmed glasses with no lenses (which he pushed up on his nose before he put the car in gear) and seagull feathers in his hair. He almost immediately drove us into a ditch.

ANNE LAMOTT
HARD LAUGHTER (1980)

goon. And perhaps she would find the company of other bird-watchers.

Adrianne White quickly became attached to the people, the community, especially the young people, many of whom lived near her on the mesa. White loved their hopeful visions. She became an active member of the community, working with several local organizations. White is glad to tell you about *her* activities in the community, "But you should talk to other people," she says, bringing out sheafs of *The Hearsay News*, B-PUD mailers, the Bolinas Plan, and a county report on how the people of Marin handled the drought of the late 1970s. "Talk to the poets. You know Bolinas is famous for its poets and writers.

"Joanne Kyger is here. Used to be married to Gary Snyder. Tom Clark *was* here. And Ferlinghetti. Aram Saroyan is here—he has a wife and two little girls, Strawberry and Cream, and a son, Armanak. Duncan McNaughton lives here. Ran for the school board and dropped out before the election because he was afraid he'd never get any more poetry written. I'm not really sure why they all came. Most of us came here to get away from other things." White laughs to herself. "We have a lot of trends in Bolinas." She pauses. "Last year it was having babies. We had about thirty women who decided all at once to have babies. Sometimes the fathers were around, sometimes they weren't. Some of the mothers have trust funds. Trust funds and food stamps help a lot. I see one mother strolling her child in an English Queen Anne pram that the grandparents sent. It's wonderful."

White laughs again. "This year's trend is young women professors who didn't get promoted into higher academic positions at Yale. Not just Yale. All the Ivy League colleges. For some reason they all wound up in Bolinas."

White's smile fades; she rubs a red spot underneath her glasses. "A lot of my young friends are leaving Bolinas now. Real-estate prices are soaring. Everything is more expensive than it used to be, and they're tired of being poor. I'll miss them.

"But I always encourage them to leave. If they can get better jobs, make a living, I'm glad. Bolinas is a bit of a dream world. I think they should move on when it's time."

She sips her cup of coffee. "The new arrivals aren't as enter-

EARLY MEMORIES OF BOLINAS

In those days there was more sea life to watch than one sees now. Sometimes, from our cottage window, we could see whales blowing and spouting, a few hundred feet beyond the breakers. . . . There were bonfires on the beach in the evenings, with singing to banjos and guitars, and hot chocolate made over the fire. Occasionally, before the bonfire, we would go for a swim by moonlight. It was an eery experience, for the waves magnified by the moonlight, looked mountainous as they approached us. But it was exciting and exhilarating, and the hot chocolate tasted better than ever.

MABEL DODGE BULLIS
EARLY MEMORIES OF BOLINAS (1974)

SHERIFF'S CALL

A street person told deputies a woman threatened him with a pipe, saying she was "tired of those negative attitudes." A man with her took the pipe and demanded, "You vagrants leave town, so we don't have to look at you on Saturday." The victim fled in his car while the man shook the pipe at him.

POINT REYES LIGHT
DECEMBER 24, 1980

taining, though. A larger percentage of them seem to be professionals from San Francisco. Commuters. They have more money, but . . ."

She stops. White is not one to find fault or criticize. She herself may leave Bolinas one day. "It's not a good place for older people. The hills are hard to climb. Health care is almost nonexistent. The older you get"—her words are slower—"the more complex your physical problems. Seniors need specialists. . . ." She drifts off, gazing at the tall waves of blue echium rustling in her garden. Quickly she stands up, looks at the clock on the wall. "Marin County is a complicated place to write about." Her shoulders seem to droop. "We like to think we live the simple life."

Bolinas Lagoon

Fishing boat, Bolinas Wharf

Above Muir Beach

MUIR BEACH

Beachside home

The Pelican Inn

Hillside home

Mailboxes

Art Center

Stinson Beach from Panoramic Highway

Stinson Beach

Superette, Highway One

Stinson Beach State Park

Bolinas Lagoon

Snowy egret, Bolinas Lagoon

Wharf Road, Bolinas

Rancho Baulenes

Chapter 3 _____ Narrow Waters

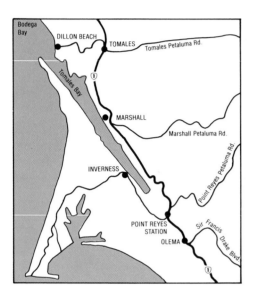

Tomales Bay (From Inverness)
Olema and Point Reyes Station
Marshall
Tomales
Dillon Beach

Tomales Bay (From Inverness)

The small pier at Inverness crawls uncertainly into the cold water of Tomales Bay. The pilings splay out at odd angles, and an abandoned dory sinks into the low-tide mud. Yellow petals from a scrubby Scotch broom drift across the weathered planks. Many years have passed since a fishing boat unloaded a catch of salmon here or a summer visitor from the old Inverness Hotel watched the herons feed in the eelgrass along the shore. But little seems to have changed since Mexican, Irish, and, later, Yankee settlers came to this rural area, where they encountered the Hookooeko Miwok people living peacefully along the bayshores and creeks.

Today a special silence still lingers. From this unassuming pier you can see the entire south end of Tomales Bay. Across the water, at Millerton, cows still graze at postcard-perfect intervals, as they did in the nineteenth century, when Swiss-Italian farmers, many sponsored by their Alpine villages, opened dairies here. Brightly painted boathouses lean lazily against the shore, like loose socks falling into comfortable boots. Tomales Bay is a silver link, the bracelet of water that holds two sister land masses together: the Point Reyes Peninsula on the west and mainland Marin on the east. It's a moving mirror of light, a twelve-and-a-half-mile dagger between two continental plates. Beneath the calm, protected bay, giant jaws of rock gnash together. "Earthquake Bay" is the name historian Jack Mason has given the place where the San Andreas Fault marries two shores, yet holds them apart. The water threatens and beckons, riding the earth in a dangerous dance between the sloping hills of the eastern shore and the dark, green ridges of the west. Beyond Inverness Ridge, on the Point Reyes Peninsula, the Pacific makes its presence known. You cannot hear the ocean, but you feel it. You smell it in the air, you are touched by its wet fingers.

Tomales Bay from Inverness

UNDER THE SECOND MOON

**Under the second moon the
Salmon come, up Tomales
Bay, up Paper Mill Creek, up
The Narrow gorge to their spawning
Beds in Devil's Gulch. Although
I expect them, I walk by the
Stream and hear them splashing and
Discover them each year with
A start.**

KENNETH REXROTH
From THE DRAGON AND THE UNICORN
(1955)

BATHING AT INVERNESS

**Besides its many rural attractions there are
more than six miles of sand beach at Inverness, and the tide on going out exposes the
sand to the sun, which warms the water on
its return, and insures delightful bathing
during the summer.**

HELEN BINGHAM
IN TAMAL LAND (1906)

Quarantine notice, Inverness

You pull your coat closer to you as a ribbon of fog unwinds from the north and hovers above Tomales Bay. The hum of an engine distracts you. A chain saw cutting lumber far up the bay at the Marshall Boatworks? You wonder for a moment if it is 1875 and the gleaming engine of the North Pacific Coast Railroad is pulling its string of buttercup-colored coaches along the narrow-gauge track from Sausalito to Tomales Bay. You can almost see the train bouncing along the wobbling trestles, swaying up the bay's eastern shore to pick up butter and shellfish at Marshall, potatoes at Tomales. Is it the "picnic run," carrying sightseers to the inns and hunting lodges of the San Geronimo Valley, of Olema, of Tomales Bay? Once, only horsedrawn wagons and schooners linked this area to the rest of the county. The railroad changed all that, opening West Marin to commerce and tourism.

"Hello." A voice startles you. A teenager in blue jeans and a plaid shirt stands near you. He pulls a pack of cigarettes from his pocket. Blond hair curls over his ears and a pencil of yellow grows above his lip. You ask if he knows where the engine noise is coming from. It's herring season, he tells you. From January to March, heavy equipment across the bay sucks the fish out of seine nets, spewing them into refrigerated crates along the shore. The herring are exported mostly to Japan, he says, where the roe is eaten as a delicacy.

You look north. The boy follows your gaze.

"Can't see Marshall from here. Get a view from Tomales Bay State Park, a few miles north of here. Nice beaches—Pebble, Indian, Heart's Desire."

Heart's Desire—a good name for the sheltered curve of sand that was slated for a housing development in the 1940s. The twisted limbs of virgin bishop pines on the cliffs above the cove still belong to the spotted owls, horned larks, and summer warblers.

"Those beaches are the best places to swim on Point Reyes Peninsula," offers the boy. "Not too much fog, no undertow. The water's warm . . . for here."

A seagull squeals suddenly and wheels into the air. Another gull has robbed him of a piece of bread picked from a garbage can behind the pier. The boy laughs. You wonder what teenagers were like sixty-five years ago, when Inverness was a remote summer resort on the southwest bay shore. Would he

Docks, Inverness

TOMALES BAY STATE PARK—IT DIDN'T JUST HAPPEN

First they [the Marin Conservation League] had an engineer survey the property to find a good first purchase in the Tomales Bay area. They picked out the 190-acre Shell Beach.

They collected $15,000 and only then they went to the board of supervisors and said, would you match these funds?

Then the league convinced state park commissioners that Shell Beach and other nearby lands were of state quality. Commissioners agreed to buy the property if they received one-half the funds needed from nonstate sources.

So the league persuaded the county to give Shell and Stinson beaches and matching funds of $26,000 to the state in 1948.

The state then bought an 840-acre parcel in the area for $150,000. In 1951, the area became Tomales Bay State Park.

MARY SUMMERS
As quoted by REBECCA LARSEN IN THE
INDEPENDENT JOURNAL
OCTOBER 8, 1974

have worked for Ben's Auto Stage, helping Ben taxi summer guests from Point Reyes Station to the hotel and cottages in Inverness? Might he have been a milker at the Pierce Ranch on Tomales Point, or an attendant at the Point Reyes Life Saving Station?

The boy turns. You watch him walk down the pier and cross the mud lot toward the Inverness garage. He stops to pat a mangy German shepherd with a gentleness that surprises you. Perhaps that's the way Julia Shafter Hamilton would have done it in 1900. Julia, heir to a large tract of land on this side of the bay, proposed a subdivision of ten thousand "villa sites" in an effort to make a profit off the land she inherited from her father, Judge James Shafter. But the 1906 earthquake knocked some of her property into the bay and shook the confidence of investors. The tiny summer town, with its one-level storefronts and sleepy cottages, was left as it was.

Earthquake. You shiver. How could such giant rumblings occur in this peaceful place? How will they change its future? Unconcerned by your musings, three black cormorants glide across the waves beyond the pier. The fog moves closer. Your feet thud against the peeling planks. You pick a yellow spray of the Scotch broom by the dock and twist it in your fingers.

In 1964, the Marin County Planning Department published a long-range plan for West Marin. The Preliminary Master Plan, as it was called, envisioned this section of the county as a booming bedroom community for San Rafael and San Francisco. Tract housing would speckle the ridges of the Point Reyes Peninsula. Along the ribs of Black Mountain at Point Reyes Station, "estate developments" would be constructed. The nearby town of Olema was slated for "cluster" housing. An airstrip, shopping centers, and high-rise condominiums would replace a dairy ranch. The population of the area, then less than 2,400, would escalate to its "ultimate holding capacity" of 66,000 shortly after the year 2000. Meanwhile, a multi-million-dollar tourist industry would provide income for West Marin.

All this new growth would be made possible by a superhighway connecting San Rafael to Point Reyes Station, with another leg extending west from Novato. Many county residents, appalled by the highway plan, began convincing plan-

OLEMA—A HAMLET OF ANOTHER ERA

The reason for Olema—if there must be a reason—is that two roads, the Coast and Sir Francis Drake, having wound for miles up and down the contours of west Marin, converge at this point.

The reason for anyone stopping at this point (reining in, as it would have been in mid-19th-century days) is something else again—at first perhaps nothing more than the custom of crossroads.

But people did stop during the last century: At one time Olema boasted three hotels, an indeterminate number of saloons, a race track, a butcher shop and a reputation for "rowdyism" heralded by a newspaper headline writer of the era.

BLAKE GREEN
SAN FRANCISCO CHRONICLE
JULY 24, 1980

Feed store, Point Reyes Station

ners and county officials that a giant asphalt slash through the San Geronimo Valley would ruin the landscape that made the area attractive. Thanks to conservationists, the suburban dream never got off its feet. The new plan for West Marin prohibits high-density development and encourages the preservation of productive agricultural land.

Olema and Point Reyes Station

A cow pasture grew to be a railroad town in the 1870s, when the North Pacific Coast Railroad built a depot there. Olema Station, as Point Reyes Station was first called, soon had its own saloon, hotel, warehouses, and general store. Once one of Marin's busiest towns, Olema itself, already dozing on the sleepy banks of Paper Mill Creek, yawned deeper when the railroad passed it by. A sorry fate for the town whose most prominent resident was the railroad's president—James M. Shafter.

Adding insult to injury, in 1891 the county renamed Olema Station, calling it Point Reyes Station. Today this name still causes confusion. Many visitors expect to find the town on the Point Reyes Peninsula; instead, it's the gateway to the eastern shores of Tomales Bay. It's the largest town in West Marin, and many of its shops are located in the old railroad buildings.

The Station House Café is a social hub of the town. Asparagus ferns hang from the long windows, and dark oak beams support the low ceilings. Pink-cheeked women in beaded shawls chat and drink coffee as they spoon ice cream to children dangling from high chairs. The café doors swing open and a dairy rancher in high milking boots stops in to trade stories with other local ranchers, who tip back their chairs at the long center table and sigh over the latest headlines from the *San Francisco Chronicle*.

With its wide main street and vintage storefronts, Point Reyes Station feels like an Old West movie set with a New Age style. At the Dance Palace, local poets and performers entertain on weekends, and a one-room clapboard structure on the edge of town houses the local anti-nuke group, the Pelican Alliance. The *Point Reyes Light* is a small weekly newspaper with offices on the south end of town. Its owners, Cathy and Dave Mitchell, recently won a Pulitzer Prize for their investigation of Synanon, a drug-and-alcohol rehabilita-

HUNTING SHARKS ON TOMALES BAY

A San Diego marine amusement park has set up camp at a Marshall boatworks to go hunting for great white sharks in Tomales Bay.

Sea World, Inc. believes it has equipment sophisticated enough to keep a great white shark in captivity—a scientific breakthrough. The Steinhart Aquarium in San Francisco last month failed with a Tomales Bay shark....

Ideally Sea World wants a young shark between four and six feet long. The company chose Tomales Bay because female great whites separate themselves and go into the bay to bear pups every summer.

POINT REYES LIGHT
SEPTEMBER 11, 1980

MARICULTURE ON TOMALES BAY

In this eerie and often foggy scene, two fishermen dressed in black wet suits slowly trudge through the lanky eel grass pulling a 40-foot net collecting an unusual catch: sea worms, crustaceans, mollusks and small fish worth up to $4 apiece to labs in need of usable specimens for environmental impact tests.

"We picked this spot to begin our business because this bay is still unpolluted," said Robert Rezina, 26, who along with Ian Campbell, 27, started their unusual fishing enterprise a year ago while they completed masters degrees in marine biology at the University of the Pacific's Dillon Beach field station.

GEORGE SNYDER
SAN FRANCISCO CHRONICLE
NOVEMBER 15, 1980

tion center that located its headquarters near Marshall, at the old Marconi Wireless Station, in 1964. Just about everyone in the area has a word to say about Synanon, some speaking warmly of its contributions to the community, others sharply critical of its leadership and practices.

Marshall

Highway 1 winds along the eastern shore of Tomales Bay, dipping through coastal ravines, then rising onto higher land. Below, small clusters of clapboard cabins extend into the water on toothpick-like stilts. Across the bay, Inverness Ridge rises like the side of a sleeping woman, covered in a green quilt of bay laurel and Douglas firs.

The bay's western shores and beaches are popular clam beds, and the biome favorable to clams also provides the bay with a unique industry—mariculture—principally oyster farming, first introduced to the area in 1875, when two foresighted entrepreneurs planted seventeen freight cars of East Coast oysters in the tidelands of Millerton.

Several oyster farms still operate along the bay, importing Pacific seed oysters, which hang on racks in the shallow waters until they reach maturity one to one-and-a-half years later. One company, International Shellfish, freshens Maine lobsters and Blue Point oysters from the East Coast in large, filtered-seawater tanks near Millerton. Barbecued oysters are a specialty at the seafood restaurants in the area. Lately there's been talk of some new oyster farms opening, and most of the fishermen up here are eager to know who'll get the permits and how many acres California Fish and Game will allot them.

Not all Tomales Bay residents work so closely with the land and water. There are writers and artists, carpenters, jewelers, potters, and rock musicians. The Youngbloods used to practice in an old barn near Marshall. Steve Miller was a longtime resident of Inverness, Jesse Colin Young still is, and occasionally former members of the Quicksilver Messenger Service drop into the Marshall Tavern to see if their tunes are still on the jukebox.

The town of Marshall, like so many on Tomales Bay, really grew up with the railroad, although its first residents, Alexander Marshall and his brothers, came twenty years before the

DISCRIMINATION AGAINST COAST MIWOKS?

For veracity's sake we must aver that the California Indian was anything but an easy subject for civilization. Knowledge he had none; his religion or morals were of the crudest form, while all in all he was the most degraded of mortals. He lived without labor, and existed for naught save his ease and pleasure. In physique he was unprepossessing, being possessed of much endurance and strength; his features were unattractive, his hair in texture like the mane of the horse, and his complexion as dark as the Ethiop's skin. His chief delight was the satisfying of his appetite and lust, while he lacked courage enough to be warlike, and was devoid of that spirit of independence, usually the principal characteristics of his race. The best portion of his life was passed in sleeping and dancing. . . .

ALLEY, BOWEN AND COMPANY
HISTORY OF MARIN COUNTY, CALIFORNIA (1880)

MIWOK INDIANS TODAY

Juanita and Sam Carrio are among dozens of Coastal Miwok descendants scattered around West Marin and just across the Sonoma County line above Tomales Bay. . . . A question put to Mrs. Carrio about an unframed painting near the kitchen table provokes a flood of stories delivered rapid-fire, punctuated by laughter, about the life of Miwoks raised in the tiny Tomales Bay homes sketched on the unframed canvas. . . . "This young generation," she says worriedly, "they've never had much of a chance. The Indian kids I work with in the schools have such hard times. . . . People act like they don't expect much of Indian kids and it's wrong, it's got to change."

ROB BAKER
PACIFIC SUN
MARCH 21–27, 1980

railroad. The Irish family traveled across the Great Plains in 1854; they were squatters, and by 1870 they owned over eight thousand acres between Marshall and Tomales. The most colorful member of the family may have been Fannie Marshall, who punched cattle, kept the family books, gave birth to three children, nursed ailing relatives, and died tired in 1861.

A lot of the old houses and stores at Marshall have gone up in flames since the early days, but if you walk a few doors down from the Marshall Tavern, you'll see one building that survived. It belongs to Bob Darr, a boatbuilder. Darr is independent, skilled at his work, and devoted to Tomales Bay. A small sign on the door of his boathouse reads, "This is a workplace. Visiting occurs on Sundays and after hours." Life up here is casual, and local folks like to drop in on each other. Darr's shop, reaching out into the cove at Marshall, is a particularly appealing gathering place. The sweet smell of sawdust greets you like an old friend; his front windows overlook the cove at Marshall—blue water, sky, and a few skiffs at anchor.

Darr is in his early thirties. His love of the sea goes back to childhood, when his father owned and skippered a schooner between San Francisco and Tahiti. Half of Bob's childhood was spent in the South Pacific, the rest in southern Marin. When he's not building boats, Darr fishes commercially—mostly for perch—and he wouldn't mind having a herring license. Herring are the bay's cash crop, bringing in some three million dollars a year.

Today, Dave, a young friend of Bob's, is helping measure the planks for the hull of an English cutter, which looms above the studio like the ribcage of a humpbacked whale. While they break for lunch, the two men talk about Marin County in the "old days," when they were kids.

"Mill Valley," says Bob, cutting a hunk of cheese, "was a little village in the 1950s. You could rent a room for twenty-five dollars a month and nobody bothered you. Just a few summer visitors. Not so many pushy corporate types. In the sixties, it was the center of the music scene."

Dave, who grew up in Point Reyes Station, was barely a year old in 1960. But his Marin has changed too. "More people here now," he says, gulping a glass of milk, "but people get along pretty well. At Tomales High the 'stoners' and ranch kids used to keep separate. The ranchers were the jocks, not the

Tomales, 1898

The Marshall Tavern

PROPOSITION 20—THE CALIFORNIA COASTAL ZONE CONSERVATION COMMISSION

27001. The people of the State of California hereby find and declare that the California coastal zone is a distinct and valuable natural resource belonging to all the people and existing as a delicately balanced ecosystem; that the permanent protection of the remaining natural and scenic resources of the coastal zone is a paramount concern to present and future residents of the state and nation . . . and that to protect the coastal zone it is necessary. . . to create the California Coastal Zone Conservation Commission, and six regional coastal zone conservation commissions, to implement the provisions of this division.

PASSED BY THE VOTERS OF CALIFORNIA IN NOVEMBER 1972

scholars. Now the ranch kids go to college too, and a lot of the 'longhairs' want to get back to the land." Dave laughs. He himself has left the land. Moved to Seattle. Someday he'd like to have a boat shop of his own, but with real-estate prices rising along Tomales Bay, he doubts he could afford it here.

The conversation wanders from boatbuilding to Synanon to sharks. Tomales Bay has a reputation for its sharks; the great white shark—"You know, the kind in *Jaws*," pipes Dave—may give birth to its young in the bay. But neither Dave nor Bob can remember a shark attack here. A couple of divers were attacked at Tomales Point, but that's no surprise, because big sharks like to hang around rocky points all along the coast.

"Mostly it's a myth," says Bob. "If you capsize, the cold water is more likely to kill you than a shark." Bob apologizes because he doesn't have long to talk. An analyst from the California Coastal Commission in San Rafael is coming to investigate a complaint about the noise made by the machines that pump herring out of the fishing boats. The herring enter the bay at evening high tide, so the machines run late into the night when the fleet is fishing. Some of the fish packers have trailers parked along the shore, and Bob thinks the commission may consider them a violation of residential zoning laws.

Dave shrugs. As far as he's concerned, the Coastal Commission has too much power already. Established by a state referendum in 1972 to protect California's coastline, it can overrule any kind of construction on coastal shores, from a major subdivision to the addition of a new toilet in an existing home. New buildings have to meet many standards, among them adequate sewage disposal, appropriate use of existing water supplies, easy public access to the shore, compatibility with historical landmarks or archeological sites, and aesthetic suitability. Dave admits the commission has done a lot to protect the coast from piecemeal development, but he also knows that the guidelines have caused problems for local property owners.

Bob is impatient. "You want houses every six feet? Another Mill Valley in West Marin?" A knock on the door ends the discussion. Steve, a Coastal Commission analyst, and Pat, the photographer, have arrived.

Bob leads the group outside to look over the herring pumps and the trailers. On the way, we pass the Marshall Tavern,

TO 'FRISCO BY SCHOONER

They came and went in greater numbers than anyone supposes, carrying produce to San Francisco markets from Point Reyes and Tomales Bay....

There were plenty of wharves—John Keys' at Tomales, Lairds Landing and Pierce's Wharf on Tomales Bay, and Sam Taylor's Embarcadero on Paper Mill Creek, to name a few....

The fatality rate was high both for boats and men. When the _Fourth of July_ was wrecked on February 20, 1878, all aboard died. Once the _Ida_ put a boat ashore for butter; the oarsman slipped in the gunwale, fell into the estero and drowned.

JACK MASON
POINT REYES HISTORIAN
WINTER 1978

Tomales Presbyterian Church

perched on the edge of the water. Buildings like this one were often part of bootlegging operations during Prohibition. Local farmers smuggled Canadian whiskey into the bay from boats outside the U.S. coastal limits, then hoisted the contraband through trapdoors into buildings along the shore. Some ranchers made their own mash and stored it in cow barns until they could transport it to San Francisco and Oakland.

Steve doesn't think the fishing trailers are violating any Coastal Commission ordinances, and Pat, the photographer, wants to know more about bootlegging.

Bob sighs. "Talk to the ranchers around here. Some of their families made fortunes from bootlegging. Whiskey paid for more barns than milk did."

The sun bursts from behind a cloud, casting silver light on the water. The trailers and pumps glisten in the bright afternoon sun. Dave heads back to the boatworks. Bob lingers behind with the commission folks.

Tomales

About four miles north of Marshall, Route 1 turns inland and follows Walker Creek two miles northeast to the town of Tomales. In the 1870s, Tomales was second in size and importance to San Rafael, the county seat. Tomales was a squatter town, settled by Irish immigrants who gambled that Mexican claims to this land would be ignored after the Mexican-American War in 1848. Although the Treaty of Guadalupe Hidalgo upheld Mexican land titles, U.S. courts often did not, and the new arrivals turned Tomales into a boomtown, known for hard drinking and boisterous bar fights. Potatoes were the cash crop. Later, dairy and sheep ranches dotted the hills rising from Tomales Bay. Schooners like John Keys's _Spray_ sailed up Walker Creek, then known only as Keys Creek, and shipped butter and potatoes out the bay and down the treacherous coast of the Point Reyes Peninsula to San Francisco. The North Pacific Coast Railroad reduced the need for that dangerous voyage when it opened its line from Sausalito to Tomales and north to the Russian River. Just in time too. Keys/Walker Creek was quickly silting up with runoff from the potato farms, and by 1880 it was inaccessible to deep-draft vessels.

Like many of the villages in this area, Tomales is closely

APHRODISIAC RANCH

Although the State Fish and Game commissioners' petition last October denied a request by San Francisco exporter Jung T. Wang for permission to establish a controversial ranch for raising and breeding Rocky Mountain elk on a 300-acre property near Tomales Bay in Marin County—for the purposes of harvesting the antlers of herbivores and selling them to Asian men who prize their supposedly aphrodisiac properties— a new hearing at the State Building in San Francisco produced a vote of 3–2 in the Korean-born Wang's favor.

SAN FRANCISCO CHRONICLE
JANUARY 14, 1978

HOW TO AVOID THE "SNEAKER WAVE"

Local boatmen advise—"Before the tide starts going out . . . be on your way in." The boatman who finds his return cut off by rough water should be prepared to remain outside until the rough water subsides, or go to another harbor such as Bodega. . . . Local boatmen say that the sudden appearance of breakers in a calm sea is common. Because such waves appear with little warning, they are called "sneaker waves."

STATE OF CALIFORNIA
DEPARTMENT OF NAVIGATION AND
OCEAN DEVELOPMENT
BOATING SAFETY HINTS FOR TOMALES BAY

linked with Petaluma, sixteen miles east in Sonoma County. San Rafael, Marin's county seat, is a twenty-four-mile trek. But that's not the only reason. Ranching, once the economic base of West Marin, continues to decline; for feed and other supplies, dairymen have no choice but to go to Sonoma.

Today, Tomales feels a little like a ghost town. The Depression hit its farmers hard, and the closing of the railroad in 1930 further isolated the community. Unless you're a student at Tomales High, the regional school for Tomales Bay and Point Reyes Peninsula, you probably won't stay too long in Tomales. The occasional tourist may pause at the Catholic and Presbyterian churches built in the 1860s, then pick up supplies at Diekmann's grocery. But most folks simply turn west at the crossroads and head for Dillon Beach, or continue north on Route 1, passing near the early railroad settlement of Fallon and on through the remote, foggy hills of northern Marin.

Dillon Beach

Dillon Beach has always been a summer town. In 1868, George Dillon, a swaggering, generous Irishman, purchased the land, and by 1888 he was inviting his friends to visit his hotel on the bluff overlooking Tomales Bay to the south, and Bodega Bay and the Pacific to the west. Today, Dillon's house continues to be the center of town life, although Dillon himself would scarcely recognize it. A large sign on the roof announces that the place is Lawsons Store, the only store in Dillon, and one of the many properties owned and operated by the Lawson family, who came to the area in the 1920s and now run the campsite, boat landing, beach, trailer camp, and a handful of rental cottages.

The weather here does not exactly constitute a summer paradise. In June, July, and August, when the tiny one-level cottages swell with vacationing families, fog envelops the town almost every day. But if you're from Sacramento, Yolo County, or the San Joaquin Valley, as many of Dillon's visitors are, the cool Pacific air is a welcome relief from the burning sun of the interior, where the daytime temperature rises well above one hundred degrees.

"We only get nice people here," says Helen Lawson, who runs the store with her husband, a professional fisherman out of Bodega. From her office behind the checkout counter, Helen

Sandstone Bluffs, Dillon Beach

Fishing pier, Lawsons Landing

manages a small empire: the store, the private beach, the rental cottages, and the trailer camp. "We don't have any bars or restaurant here," she says, lighting a cigarette. "So people who want to raise hell stay away. Then there's the weather." She emerges from her office to arrange a dusty rack of suntan oil and talk to Betty, her friend and check-out clerk.

"You have to be a special kind of person to put up with the weather here. The water's too cold for swimming, and if you don't like to fish there's not much to do."

"In the old days," says Lawson, watching a grade-school boy select a candy bar, "we were the only people here in winter. We were never lonely, though. Always plenty to do." Lawson doesn't exactly recall what they *did* do in the old days, but she has an especially fond memory of her grandmother. Once every season she took her upright piano down to the beach on a pickup truck, and the summer guests—most of them were friends—joined the family for sing-alongs.

Lawson doesn't dwell on the past; but the future of the business is often on her mind. She'd like to expand, maybe build a restaurant and more trailer facilities on the bluff.

"Tell the story about the Coastal Commission," says Betty, smiling. "You know, the time you went down to the hearing in San Rafael and they thought Dillon Beach was in Sonoma."

Lawson scowls. Suddenly, Betty runs to the window overlooking the beach. "Look, quick. A whale spouting just beyond the breakers." Before Helen can spot the spume, a Granny Goose Potato Chips truck pulls into the lot and obstructs the view. Betty laughs. The phone rings and Helen disappears into her office.

Beyond Lawsons parking lot, a narrow road winds down past the summer houses and dips toward the beach. On this day there is no fog, only blue sky and wisps of cirrus clouds. The surf rolls onto the long, wide beach, leaving bubbles of foam on the wet sand. The wind blusters and roars, shaking the dune grass. To the north, granite stacks and the tidepools, for which Dillon is famous, mark the beach's end. One white curl of foam shows the hideout of the "sneaker wave." At the mouth of Tomales Bay, where the ocean floor rises from two hundred feet to ten feet, the great wave has smacked the hulls of many unsuspecting boats, dashing them against the hidden sandbar below.

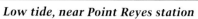
Low tide, near Point Reyes station

T

View from Inverness

Boathouse

INVERSION

"Downtown" Inverness

Inverness Library

Lagunitas/Paper Mill Creek

OLEMA

Bear Valley

Druid Hall

Grocery

Point Reyes Station from Inverness Ridge

Ranch hands

POINT REYES STATION

JOHN LUND

Marshall

Commercial fishing boats

Marshall Boatworks

St. Helen's Catholic Church

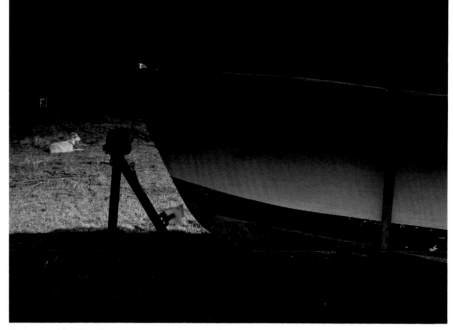

Front yard, Hamlet

Cabin, Hamlet

Piers, Nicks Cove

Church of the Assumption

Diekmann's General Store

TOMALES

Tidal flats, Tomales Bay

DILLON BEACH

Tomales Point from Dillon Beach

Cabins, Dillon Beach

Lawsons Store

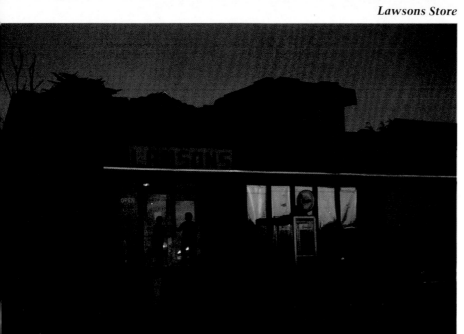

Part 2

Fog over Tamalpais ridges

MID-MARIN: The Interior Land

Chapter 4 ___ In the Shadow of the Mountain

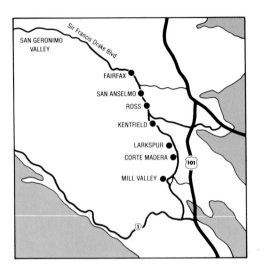

Mill Valley
Corte Madera
Larkspur
Ross Valley **(Kentfield/Ross,
San Anselmo and Fairfax)**
San Geronimo Valley

Mill Valley

Mill Valley is not as old as Bolinas, lacks Sausalito's waterside charm, can boast of no grand dairy ranches as are common in West Marin or the northern hills of Novato. What Mill Valley has is a mountain. The southern Marin town is at the foot of Mount Tamalpais, winding up redwood canyons to secluded ridges overlooking the slopes of the mountain to the blue reaches of San Francisco Bay.

Downtown Mill Valley is nestled between two creeks. On the north is what some residents call "the little creek with the big name"— Arroyo Corte Madera del Presidio. On the south is Old Mill Creek, where John Reed built the county's first sawmill in 1836. Because of the creeks, the long shadows cast by the mountain, and the coastal fog that drifts up Richardson Bay from the southeast, the town is cooler in the summer than many parts of interior Marin.

The streets of Mill Valley spread out from the old railroad depot like the petals of a sunflower. Bay laurels and second-growth redwoods rise above the sidewalks, inviting friends and neighbors to linger in the shade. In Varney's Hardware on Throckmorton, at the Mill Valley Market on Corte Madera Avenue, residents stop to laugh about last night's variety show at the Odd Fellows' Hall and the "Fill the Kitty" fund to support the black and white cat who lives on the deck of the public library. Outside Living Foods Inc., a gray-haired woman in a huge straw hat hands the manager a poster announcing a series of nature walks she is leading on Mount Tamalpais.

And the mountain speaks in every conversation, often silently, her looming presence as much a part of life as sunshine or summer fog. A serene energy emanates from Tamalpais, and many Mill Valley residents will tell you it's this energy which brought them here. Whether they jog and hike

Summer fog, Mill Valley

Home near Panoramic Highway, Mill Valley

JOHN LUND

Falch House, Mill Valley

ABOVE MILL VALLEY

I've come home from Trout Fishing in America, the highway bent its long smooth anchor about my neck and then stopped. Now I live in this place. It took my whole life to get here, to get to this strange cabin above Mill Valley.

RICHARD BRAUTIGAN
TROUT FISHING IN AMERICA (1967)

on the mountain's trails, or simply gaze at her peaks from the warmth of a redwood hot-tub, residents respect the mountain. And it's always been that way. Long ago, the Coast Miwok Indians worshipped Tamal, building huts along her bayshore creeks. In 1873, before Mill Valley was a town, San Francisco's Dr. John Cushing brought his patients to Tamalpais to recuperate at his health spa in Blithedale Canyon.

Cushing's "discovery" led others to build summer cabins at the mountain's foot. The site so impressed San Francisco developer Joseph Eastland that he laid out a town here. In May 1890 the Tamalpais Land and Water Company, headed by Eastland, auctioned hundreds of lots in what is now downtown Mill Valley, on land once a part of William Richardson's Rancho Saucelito. A spur-line train connected Eastland, as the town was sometimes called, with Sausalito and the ferries bound for San Francisco.

By 1896, visitors were flocking to Mill Valley to hike on Tamalpais and ride "the crookedest railroad in the world," a narrow-gauge line zigzagging up to the Tavern on Mount Tam's East Peak. Trains dropped as many as a thousand people an hour at the depot. The town's streets, reported one newspaper, were "thronged on some weekends with crowds of excursionists and toughs . . . the tinkle of bottles flying off the mountain train was a familiar sound."

"What saved us from becoming another Sausalito," recalls Sam Bagshaw, who, as a boy, helped his Welsh parents run their grocery and restaurant catering to the tourist trade, "was the development of resorts on the Russian River in Sonoma. Almost overnight, the crowds disappeared." Instead of becoming a town of saloons, gambling joints, and cheap hotels, Mill Valley settled into a more sedate existence, its population increasing after the 1906 earthquake, but remaining under four thousand until World War II. It was then that the growth of Mill Valley began, and it has continued ever since, with subdivisions and tract houses crawling up the mountain's ridges and sprawling out across the town's low-lying bayshore fringes.

"When you live in a community for a long time," says Jean Barnard, mayor of Mill Valley from 1972 to 1974, and great-niece of Lovell White, one of the town's original developers, "you get over the paranoia about changes." Although she's a

MILL VALLEY NOVELIST REMEMBERS

It was a great adventure, in 1891, for my mother and father to move us all to Mill Valley, once the great Throckmorton ranch, recently plotted into building lots scattered on the steep slopes of Tamalpais mountain and on the mountain chain stretching on the east and west to enclose the valley. For my father was the sole support of five unusually healthy and hungry children, his frail and clinging little sister Kitty, his wife with her fixed ideas of "niceness," which included fresh tablecloths daily, butter made into balls, children's underlinen changed three times weekly, and, of course, a cook in the kitchen and a young girl to help with beds, child care, and the Monday wash.

KATHLEEN NORRIS
FAMILY GATHERING (1954)

MARIN MONOPOLY

Sometimes Kate wondered if she and Harvey would ever move uphill. Marin Monopoly dictated that every time you made another thou after taxes, you moved and gained another hundred feet in altitude. The Harrises, for example, had made it from a hilltop in Mill Valley to a higher hilltop in San Rafael, and finally, in a pace-setting coup, back to the City, where they lived in a penthouse on Telegraph Hill.

CYRA McFADDEN
THE SERIAL (1976)

MILL VALLEY MUSICIANS & ROCK STARS
(Partial List)

Rita Abrams, Marty Barron, David Crosby, Mimi Fariña, David Grisman, Dan Hicks, Jefferson Airplane, Country Joe McDonald, Steve Miller, Maria Muldaur, Carlos Santana, Sly Stone

conservationist, Barnard doesn't share the desire of some new-comers to "pull up the drawbridge behind them" once they arrive in Marin. One change that has affected her personally is the conversion of her uncle Ralston White's Blithedale Canyon estate, "The Garden of Allah," into a retreat operated by the United Church of Christ. She is pleased that others can now marvel at the heart-shaped front lawn and experience "wisteria hysteria," an affliction Barnard's Aunt Ruth suffered from each spring, when the beauty of the lavender blossoms compelled Mrs. White to invite all her friends to wisteria-watching parties.

"People from the East are amazed by Mill Valley," says Dick Shain, a marketing consultant who works from his home above Mount Tam's Middle Ridge. "They can't believe you can live on this mountain, watch the sun rise over the bay, and commute to San Francisco in twenty minutes. But you can in Mill Valley." He grins and points to the shaggy sheep dog at his feet. "The town's so friendly that more people know Fred's name than mine."

Corte Madera

Although it's a small town, Corte Madera, like its "twin city," Larkspur, has a split personality—two climates, two types of terrain, two business districts. The split comes from the town's location: Corte Madera runs eastward from the hot foothills of Tamalpais—where the old town began—to the cool, tidal marshlands of San Francisco Bay.

In the 1830s and '40s, Corte Madera's virgin redwoods were logged by landowner John Reed, who shipped some of the timber to San Francisco via Corte Madera Creek. When California joined the Union in 1850, squatters flocked to Reed's Corte Madera *sobrante*, or "leftover," claiming 160-acre parcels under the National Homestead Act. In 1885, Frank Morrison Pixley paid Reed's daughter Hilarita two thousand dollars in gold coin to guarantee his title to Owl's Wood, a 160-acre estate given him by his father-in-law. A San Francisco attorney and politician, Pixley was also founder and editor of *The Argonaut*, a magazine whose contributors included Mark Twain, Ambrose Bierce, Gertrude Atherton, and Sausalito poet Daniel O'Connell.

Childless, Amelia and Frank Pixley left Owl's Wood to

MARIN SURVIVES THE DROUGHT

A state report on what happened in Marin during the drought confirmed what most county residents already knew—faced with a big problem, people took extreme measures to save water and survived the dry spell. . . .

The major finding of the report was that "a community can accommodate even prolonged and intense drought conditions. . . ."

Residential water use was cut by more than the 57 percent called for by the Marin Municipal district.

INDEPENDENT JOURNAL
FEBRUARY 21, 1980

THE ROSEBOWL

Larkspur is probably most remembered today for the outdoor dances held here from 1913 to 1963. The dances, first held in the small downtown park at the corner of Ward and Magnolia, were sponsored by the Larkspur Volunteer Firemen's Association to raise money for equipment and a firehouse. When they became so successful that they needed a setting of their own, they moved to the redwood grove surrounded by the rose-covered fencing adjacent to the gurgling creek.

Dancers fox-trotted, jitterbugged and waltzed on the waxed hardwood floor beneath Chinese lanterns and strings of colored lights hung from the trees. . . .

Dancers arrived from all over the Bay Area on the two-lane roads or on the ferries and the train—a one-way boat and train ticket to Larkspur was 54¢.

THE LARKSPUR HERITAGE COMMITTEE
LARKSPUR: PAST AND PRESENT (1979)

Frank's sister-in-law Emma Pixley and her sons, who created Corte Madera's first subdivision and developed the downtown.

In 1937 the closing of Frank Keever's Meadowsweet Dairy, on fourteen hundred acres of Corte Madera marshland, paved the way for the development of the bayshore. Developer Frank Rusalem purchased much of the land, opening two shopping centers and subdivisions in the 1950s and '60s.

The 1930s brought another major change to Corte Madera— the completion of U.S. Highway 101. For almost one hundred years, Marin's major overland route had run north from Sausalito through Corte Madera, Larkspur, and Ross Valley. The North Pacific Coast Railroad also followed this route, as did the electric commuter trains that ran until 1940.

Highway 101 bypassed the old valley route through Corte Madera, instead heading north along the bayshore. Today the highway contributes to the feeling that there are two Corte Maderas, one east of the highway, one west. The same phenomenon occurs in Larkspur, Greenbrae, San Rafael, Novato, and all the communities intersected by U.S. 101.

Larkspur

In the 1840s, thirty Maryland businessmen formed the Baltimore and Frederick Mining and Trading Company for the purpose of "prosecuting any and every kind of business which might be available in the new California." John Reed's redwood stands in the east canyons of Tamalpais, a few miles north of what would later become Mill Valley, appealed to the entrepreneurs. They shipped a sawmill around Cape Horn and erected it at the mouth of Baltimore Canyon, which they logged. This was the beginning of the town that would be named Larkspur in 1886, when Charles W. Wright bought six hundred acres in the area and subdivided a cattle ranch into tiny lots. Some claim that Wright's wife named the town when she mistook a blue lupine plant in the canyon for a larkspur, common to her native England.

Sunnier and drier than Mill Valley, Larkspur's sloping ridges seemed ideal for growing grapes. In 1881, Jean Escalle, a French bricklayer, saw the opportunity to make wine and opened Escalle Vineyards on Magnolia Avenue in North Larkspur. Rieslings and Zinfandels were the vineyard's specialties, which, according to the Larkspur Heritage Committee, were delivered "two or three times a week in a buggy drawn by a horse named Pedro."

Larkspur's development was boosted by the arrival of the North Pacific Coast train from Sausalito.

Leslie Ezekial remembers Larkspur at the turn of the century. "When I was a young girl living in Mill Valley," she recalls, "I was not allowed to come to Larkspur. It was called 'Jagtown' in those days and it was very rough on weekends, with all the drinking places."

By the 1920s, Larkspur's image had improved, as wealthy San Franciscans built year-'round homes in the hills above the old town. Today it remains an attractive residential community, popular with San Francisco commuters.

"Things haven't changed much in Larkspur in the last thirty years," says Larkspur real estate agent Sue Schaefer, who is part owner of the clapboard house which Larkspur's "Crazy Murphy" built in 1888. Unoccupied for many years, Murphy's house was said to be haunted, and stories of Murphy's ghost intrigued and frightened generations of Larkspur children. No longer. Today his house is Lark Creek Inn, a popular bar and restaurant; the modest summer cabins of the town's early years are prized parcels of real estate. According to Schaefer, the average price of a home in Larkspur is $167,000, which seems low, she adds, because it includes the new condominiums in Greenbrae and Skylark, developments on the town's northeastern outskirts.

"No, the town hasn't changed much at all," repeats Schaefer. "Except for the ferry terminal at Larkspur Landing and the new shops over there, it hasn't changed. I've been a member of the chamber of commerce for years and I always see the same people, same faces."

Ross Valley

Leading westward from Highway 101, past the shopping centers of Greenbrae, Sir Francis Drake Boulevard changes character when it enters Ross Valley. The trees seem older, larger, shadier; the oleander bushes and English ivy seem richer, more elegant—carefully lush. You feel you've entered an earlier era, a place that remembers genteel garden parties and the sheltered life of old money, reminiscent of East Coast

Lark Creek Inn, Larkspur

ROSS WIDOW LEAVES $260 MILLION TO MARIN COUNTY

In Marin County, it seems everybody wants a piece of the Buck bucks.

Which is no surprise, because a $250 million oil fortune can be divided into a lot of pieces.

The millions come from the estate of Beryl Buck, a Ross widow who died in 1975, specifying in her will that her money be used to benefit the people of Marin County—and no one else.

The people of Marin, who already enjoy one of the highest per capita incomes of any area in the nation, have generated an avalanche of ideas on how the money should be spent to benefit them.

San Francisco Chronicle, 1980

BOYHOOD RECOLLECTIONS OF MARIN COUNTY

I found myself in an environment of cosmopolite democracy and independence, a tolerant population without race prejudice. There were Indians and Mexicans, Chilians and "Chilenos," Hawaiians and Spaniards, and other white men from every corner of the world. The few negroes were considered as much people as anyone else. I suppose half the conversations I held outside the family were in broken English. A large part of the labor was done by Chinamen who, in spite of their unfortunately increasing numbers, were a picturesque and valued part of the population.

WILLIAM KENT
REMINISCENCES OF OUTDOOR LIFE (1929)

MELLOWSPEAK—AT COLLEGE OF MARIN

It was like, you know, mellow.

These two linguists, Jane Falk and Robin Lakoff, are into "Marin English." And they shared their feelings about "Language in the Hot Tub: Talking Mellow" with 118 people at the College of Marin last night. They acknowledged that the way people relate in Marin is okay....

Once Jane got her act together, she acknowledged: "Marin English has spread to the Hebrew and Japanese languages. They both have translations for 'where your head is at....'

"Nothing is static in Marin English," related Jane, "and the metaphors are directional—far out, where you're coming from, into.

"In the east, you are *in* **psychoanalysis. It's something serious and permanent. In Marin English, you are** *into* **est."**

GEORGE FRAZIER
INDEPENDENT JOURNAL
FEBRUARY 7, 1980

communities on Philadelphia's Main Line or Long Island's North Shore.

Kentfield, Ross, and San Anselmo blend imperceptibly into each other along Mount Tam's northeastern edge, although their personalities differ. The western portion of San Anselmo changes after Sir Francis Drake Boulevard curves sharply west toward Fairfax.

The North Pacific Coast Railroad to Tomales opened the sunny, rolling valley of Ross to San Francisco commuters. Orchards and dairy ranches became private estates. Although Golden Gate Transit buses have replaced the electric trains introduced in 1903, and many of the nineteenth-century estates have been subdivided, you can still see pinstriped bankers waiting at leaf-dappled bus stops. And the ladies lunching at the Marin Art and Garden Center in Ross would have brought a smile to the face of Emily Post herself.

Yet these people don't seem as formal as their Eastern counterparts. The financial manager may be hiking on Mount Tam in Levi's tomorrow, while the Pucci-clad mother delivers an impassioned speech to the chaplain of Marin General Hospital on the need for special counseling for rape victims and battered women.

Kentfield and Ross

Genteel iconoclasm is not new to Ross Valley. Albert Kent, owner of Chicago's largest meat-packing firm, and one of the area's early settlers, came to the valley in 1872 for health reasons. He preferred tapping Morse code messages to firms in the East from his four-hundred-acre estate to socializing with his neighbors.

Neither Adaline, Kent's wife, nor his son, William, shared his reticence. Both were community activists whose works for the county are still apparent today. Adaline donated twenty-three acres of her Kentfield property for a recreation center in 1908. Today the land is the site of the College of Marin, a vibrant and diverse educational community that stands in sharp contrast to the old grandeur around it.

Tamalpais looms above the college's central green, a wide lawn fringed with flowers. Students, backpacks resting by their feet, can be seen reading volumes from their Third World Lit class, while the women's championship basketball team

Bolinas Stage on Mount Tamalpais, 1906

CANINE CRISIS

Before long, if Marin County's love for its dogs continues, the county could face some unsolvable dilemmas and unpopular laws. Many people are literally waking up to many of the irritating and potentially dangerous dog-related problems—tons of waste, barking late into the night, packs of dogs roaming the open spaces, cruelty, poisonings, dog owners who openly flaunt the law and common sense, and the inability of local institutions to rectify the situation. Already the issue of dog control has become a hot potato that most politicians, knowing the sanctified role of the hound in Marin households, prefer to toss aside . . . .

RICHARD STEVEN STREET
PACIFIC SUN
JANUARY 4–10, 1980

**San Francisco Theological Seminary
San Anselmo**

jogs through the quad to the gym. Chances are they don't know much about Adaline Kent or the annual Sunny Hills Grape Festival she and her family hosted for forty-three years.

Marin residents are more familiar with her son William's contributions. Through William Kent's conservation efforts, much of Mount Tamalpais is a state park today rather than a tract development. In 1907, Kent donated the land for Muir Woods National Monument. And as U.S. Congressman from 1910 to 1916, he wrote and lobbied successfully for the passage of the National Park Service Act.

Most of Albert Kent's holdings in Ross Valley had belonged to James Ross, a San Francisco importer-exporter who bought Rancho Punta de Quentin from its owner, Juan Cooper, in 1857. From Ross Landing, on Corte Madera Slough, hay, timber, and dairy products were barged to Corte Madera Creek, then shipped to San Francisco. Many nineteenth-century estates were carved from Ross's property, including Sunnyside, his daughter Anne's home, built by her husband, George Worn. Eight and one-half acres of that property now belong to the Marin Art and Garden Center, founded by conservationist Caroline Livermore in 1946. The center is the workspace for thirteen nonprofit community groups; the gardens thrive under the valley's summer sun and the loving care of the center's members. The grounds manager is outspoken, seventy-seven-year-old Sara Tuckey, who can name every tree, shrub, or weed on the estate, discuss the aesthetics of dried-flower arrangements or pottery glazes, or describe the last ten weddings held in the center's reception hall. If you talk to her for long, you'll be convinced that Ross Valley starts at the entrance to the Art and Garden Center and ends at the exit.

San Anselmo

San Anselmo is the largest town in Ross Valley. The sunny storefronts and relaxed cafés, wrapped along the bend in San Anselmo Creek, attract visitors like clover honey on a croissant from Le Bistro. Weekend travelers hurrying along Sir Francis Drake Boulevard to the parks and beaches of West Marin inevitably choose to break their journey here. San Anselmo has had this effect for over one hundred years, when it was known as "the Junction," where the spur-line train from San Rafael joined the narrow-gauge to Tomales. Weekenders

Japanese garden, Sleepy Hollow

SAN ANSELMO CAFÉ

Two Beans in a Pod Café is more crowded than usual. The braided woman in the rainbow gypsy shawl mutters at the Swedish ivy, philodendron and spider plants overflowing the wooden window. Two women finger the collection of plastic bubble snow scenes on the wooden shelf; one shakes the dancing elves complaining about the problems of selling her house while the other watches the snow sympathetically, mentioning her own tenant difficulties.

And Sharon, the café owner, soothes with a tender word or a fiery insult as she pulls the steamed milk lever, stirs espresso, removes the piping blueberry muffins from the tiny oven. . . .

ABIGAIL HEMSTREET
JOURNAL ENTRY
JANUARY 27, 1981

camped in the orchards and hayfields along the creek, renting space from owner Barnard Brenfleck. The town's growth was boosted in 1892, when the San Francisco Theological Seminary constructed an imposing, turreted edifice on a hill above Shady Lane. Most of the original buildings are still used by the seminary. The presence of the Presbyterian clerics did not dampen the town's enthusiasm for "blind pigs," unlicensed saloons that flourished during Prohibition. Some old-timers still remember The Teapot, where whiskey was served in cups and saucers.

Today there is only one bar in town, but coffee shops abound. In Hilda's, on San Anselmo Avenue, you're likely to see a retired broker in a Harris tweed jacket eating his grilled-cheese sandwich next to a bearded carpenter or a flaxen-haired clerk from the gift shop next door. Meanwhile, at the Wells Fargo Bank down the street, a mother and her children stop to gaze at the giant, sepia-toned photograph of San Anselmo in the early 1900s. The kids marvel at the rolling brown field, where a handful of sheep graze undisturbed by automobiles or shopping centers—a reminder of what seems a simpler, more peaceful place and time.

Fairfax

Although Fairfax is just a mile west of San Anselmo's "hub," the town seems as Western as San Anselmo seems Eastern. Single-level wooden storefronts line the business district along Sir Francis Drake Boulevard, which is wider here, where the trains to West Marin sliced through the middle of town. Converted summer cabins and imposing suburban ranch houses cling to the hills above San Anselmo and Fairfax creeks. Beyond the town limits, the Mount Tamalpais State Game Refuge and the Marin Municipal Watershed, more than eighteen thousand acres of land, stretch southward to the peaks of Tamalpais and westward to Bolinas Ridge. No wonder that early motion picture companies shot cowboy films in the Fairfax hills before there were Hollywood backlots.

"Easygoing," "peaceful," "mellow" are words Fairfax residents use to describe their town. "It's not as built up as Tiburon," says a Fairfax mother, who recently moved here with her husband and children. "We have more space than we did in Tiburon, more privacy, and a more mixed community—

FAIRFAX EPICUREANS

Here came "Lord Fairfax" to establish a hunting lodge. You, who will remember his home in later days, presided over by the lovable Madame Pastori, and who have partaken of the epicurean feasts prepared by her husband, "Charlie," served perhaps in one of the platforms high in the massive old oaks, will be interested to know that the roses which climbed above your heads were planted by "Lady Fairfax," who brought to the wilderness her love of English flowers and gardens. In those days the wild ducks nested in the lake below the knoll, where later Mr. Carrigan was to build, and it was not uncommon for guests coming to the hospitable Fairfax home to have their mounts frightened by the bears, which lived in the forests of native laurel, madrone and oaks.

MARGO KITTLE BOYD
REMINISCENCES OF EARLY MARIN GARDENS

FAIRFAX, A.M.

We go into the house and begin that two-hour yak-yak activity we call breakfast. We sit around and bring ourselves slowly back to consciousness, treating ourselves like fine pieces of china and after we finish the last cup of the last cup of the last cup of coffee, it's time to think about lunch or go to the Goodwill in Fairfax.

RICHARD BRAUTIGAN
TROUT FISHING IN AMERICA (1967)

not just professionals and commuters, but young people and old-timers and Italian families who've owned shops and restaurants here for years."

Relaxed as it may seem today, Fairfax has had a colorful past. Back in 1861, for example, one of the last fatal pistol duels in California took place on the property of Charles Snowden Fairfax, a transplanted Virginian, whose title, had he chosen to use it, would have been Lord Fairfax, tenth Baron of Cameron.

Fairfax came to California with the Virginia Company, an Eastern outfit that mined gold in the Mother Lode during the Gold Rush. The company collapsed, but Fairfax, outfitted in velvet dress coats and ruffled shirts, threw himself into state politics. He built a house in Bird's Nest Glen, on thirty-two acres of dairy land, now the site of downtown Fairfax. He and his wife, Ada, entertained lavishly at the glen, where champagne is said to have bubbled almost as freely as the falls on Cascade Creek beside their home.

Long after the Fairfaxes were gone, the site of their estate continued to be a place of conviviality and recreation. When the narrow-gauge came through the town, hundreds of day trippers picnicked in the glen. Even more arrived in 1913 to take the five-cent funicular ride up to Fairfax Manor.

By the 1940s the funicular was gone, but the glen continued to witness some of the town's more boisterous and controversial events. The annual Fourth of July firemen's picnic in Fairfax Park was the center of a political dispute that shook the county and state. Elsa Gidlow, a poet and journalist who now lives near Muir Woods National Monument, remembers the episode clearly.

"Fairfax was something of a frontier town in the forties," she recalls. "It grew up on Prohibition and a considerable number of us—new and old Fairfax residents—were trying to reform the town government. Every year there was a Fourth of July picnic and pageant in the park. Several members of the city council were diverting funds raised by the event to themselves and their political friends and supporters. The money was needed to make necessary improvements in the town lighting and many more neglected areas." Gidlow shakes her head.

"Three vacancies on the council were coming open and we put forward and worked hard for three of our own." The

SAMUEL TAYLOR'S PAPER MILL

Not only did Taylor have difficulty in getting his supplies to the mill but in getting his product to his best customers, the San Francisco newspapers.

The lookout at the top of Telegraph Hill, who kept San Franciscans informed on the arrival and departure of ships, would be besieged by the *Alta California, The Bulletin,* **and** *The Call* **when they were short on newsprint. The query was: "Has the sloop from Bolinas yet hove in sight?"**

FLORENCE DONNELLY
MARIN COUNTY HISTORICAL SOCIETY
BULLETIN
DECEMBER 1976

Deli, Lagunitas

reformers' campaign was successful, but, says Gidlow, "When the old guard realized that we were not after 'the loot,' their only explanation for our hard work and commitment was that we were Communists."

In 1949, the California Un-American Activities Committee—known as the Tenney Committee—arrived in Fairfax to investigate Gidlow and one of the newly elected council members.

"Neither of us was even remotely Communist," she says, "although given the law of averages, there *may* have been one or two among our supporters." The committee managed to stir up a good deal of trouble, but never found any evidence that Gidlow and her colleague were Communists. With the seasoned good humor of her eighty-one years, Gidlow laughs when she recalls Stanton Delaplane's report in the *San Francisco Chronicle* headlined, "Red Linen Washed Pink at Fairfax Hearing."

Today there are still a few controversies in Fairfax, but the town seems to absorb widely differing values and lifestyles with greater ease than many Marin communities.

Some say that Fairfax is the "drug capital" of Marin County. "I'm not sure why Fairfax attracts dealers," says a resident writer who once dealt cocaine herself. "I suppose people who enjoy 'sister cocaine' also enjoy the good things of life, like beautiful surroundings and warm weather. Fairfax has a long growing season—over six months of sun—which is great for growing marijuana. I don't do that anymore, though. The paranoia's terrible. Not because of the cops, but the teenagers. They terrorize growers and rip them off at harvest time."

County Sheriff Al Howenstein has heard all this before. But as far as he can tell, Fairfax has no more drugs or restless teenagers than any other part of the county. Meanwhile, the people of Fairfax continue to accept and enjoy the diversity of their community. That, after all, is what the West is all about.

San Geronimo Valley

On the western fringe of Fairfax, Sir Francis Drake Boulevard climbs the long grade of White's Hill, an incline that was too steep for most nineteenth-century travelers in horsecarts and carriages. What visitors missed by not continuing onward was a cozy, rolling valley between the foggy sweeps of coastal

THE CABIN IN LAGUNITAS

She found a cabin in Lagunitas and bought it; borrowing the money from Henry, she would pay him back when she sold the novel. She gave herself the silence of the forest as a reward. She gave herself wild blackberry hedges for neighbors, wet ferns dripping through gray mist outside the window, squirrels clattering bay laurel branches against the window.

ABIGAIL HEMSTREET
PRIDE OF MADEIRA
(1981)

Paper Mill Creek, Samuel P. Taylor State Park

Marin and the populated towns of the interior.

Four tiny, unincorporated towns—San Geronimo, Woodacre, Forest Knolls, and Lagunitas—dot the eight-mile corridor at almost even intervals. In the rush to reach the sea, many travelers are content to pass quickly through the valley, an arrangement that agrees with some of its residents. When the trains ran, tourists flocked to the tents and picnic tables along the creek, celebrating so raucously that the local farmers were dismayed. According to Marin historian Jack Mason, one resident was most disturbed by "groups of women wearing breeches, who act like pigs, scampering half-naked among the trees, conducting revels at night and starting fires."

Hard to believe it happened in the valley once owned by Paul Revere's grandson, Joseph Warren, and later by Adolph Maillard, a grandson of King Joseph Bonaparte, Napoleon's older brother. Maillard's sister-in-law was Julia Ward Howe, who penned the words of "The Battle Hymn of the Republic."

Hoping to lure permanent residents, the Lagunitas Development Company acquired the Maillard family holdings in 1912, created the villages of Woodacre and Forest Knolls, and subdivided tracts in Lagunitas and San Geronimo. But the valley was too remote for most commuters, and many summer visitors preferred camping in Taylor Park, just west of Lagunitas, to buying property in the area. Today, Taylor Park is Samuel P. Taylor State Park, 2,576 acres of land along Paper Mill Creek, where Taylor started the West Coast's first paper mill in 1856.

Samuel P. Taylor State Park

Riding Stables, San Geronimo Valley

Blithedale Avenue

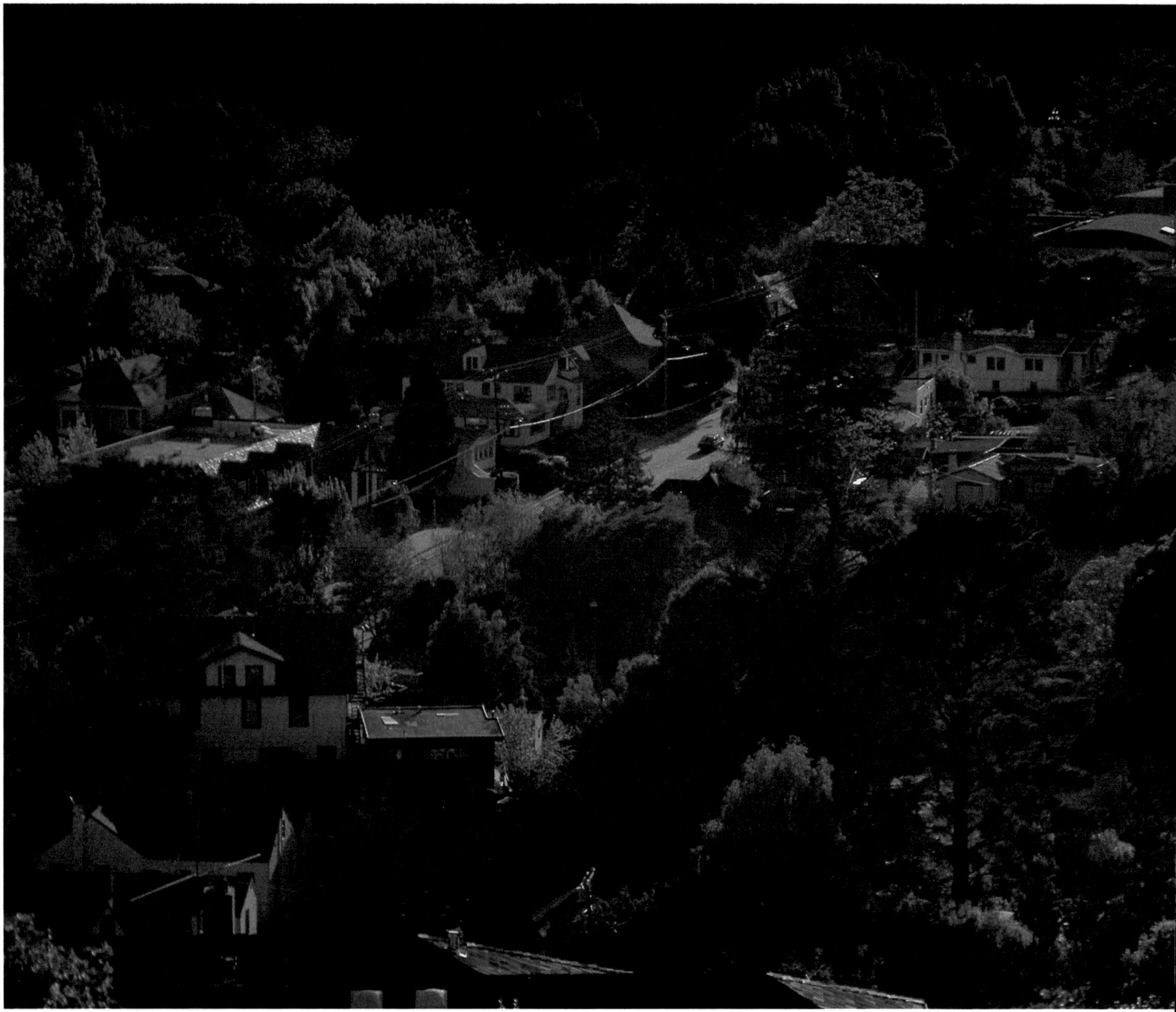

MILL VALLEY

JOHN LUND

Mill Valley Book Depot

Creekside flower stand

CORTE MADERA
and LARKSPUR

Larkspur Ferry Terminal

Condominiums, Corte Madera Creek

Corte Madera home

JOHN LUND

Shady Lane

Ross

Victorian home

Sidewalk café

Sᴀɴ ᴀɴSELMO

Sir Francis Drake Boulevard

Downtown

San Anselmo Creek *Cheda Building*

Center Boulevard shops

F<small>AIRFAX</small>

Fairfax Cinema

Navés Saloon

Chapter 5 ——————————— Pastoral Ranchlands

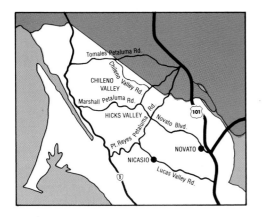

A seventeen-year-old girl in blue jeans and a plaid wool jacket stands on a grassy ridge. It is twilight. The wind blows its low, familiar cry across the hills. Susan Dolcini looks down into Hicks Valley, where her family has been dairy farming for one hundred years. The cows wait outside the rambling barn, udders full. "I wouldn't give this place up for anything," says Susan. "If something's bugging me, I can just grab a horse or go for a walk and be completely alone." Across the valley, the dinosaur ribs of Hicks Mountain seem to plant themselves deeper into the land.

Gary Giacomini leans back in his swivel chair and lights a cigarette. He drops the match into an ashtray balanced on a pile of papers on a square oak table inside his office at the Marin County Civic Center. Giacomini is the supervisor for the Fourth District of Marin County, which includes most of the county's dairy and cattle ranches. The Giacomini clan is a big one; Gary has cousins, uncles, and in-laws who ranch. "In 1972, the year I ran for election," he says, "the destiny of West Marin was really on the line. There was a big subdivision in San Geronimo Valley, there were pending subdivisions from Nicasio to Sonoma. They were everywhere. It would have resulted in 300,000 houses in West Marin. Many ranchers were ready to sell. Their feed and utility costs were going up, and they had enormous property and inheritance taxes. They weren't sure they could make a living anymore."

Giacomini tugs his mustache. "As a sort of holding action, we fought successfully to get the land zoned A-60, one house per sixty acres, to limit density. At the time the ranchers hated it. They didn't want their option to develop removed. Now most of them are for it. You know what I mean?" The two aides sitting at the table look at Giacomini fondly.

View from Wilson Hill Road

COUNTRY COUSINS

The agricultural community, in general, looked with disinterest, not disdain, at that other world of Marin. So long as their City-oriented neighbors tended to their business in San Francisco and let them mind the store in Marin, there was room for all. Let the City people build their parks, their theatres, and their resorts, that didn't hurt anybody. Not until the use of the land for those purposes began to encroach on the plans the "local" populace had for the same areas was there conflict.

DR. EVELYN MORRIS RADFORD
THE BRIDGE AND THE BUILDING (1973)

VISITING A MARIN DAIRY RANCH

My first introduction to the wild west came on a Sunday at the dairy ranch where we first lived, when a Spaniard who was half witted and over half drunk and who, although deaf and dumb, emitted discordant vocal sounds, rode a broncho to a finish. I have never seen in all subsequent experience such power to recover balance. He just couldn't fall off.

WILLIAM KENT
REMINISCENCES OF OUTDOOR LIFE (1929)

There are over seventy dairy and cattle ranches in Marin County. Most are in northern and West Marin, between Tomales Bay, Novato, and the Sonoma County line. These are the pastoral ranchlands of interior Marin—more than 100,000 acres of hills, ridges, canyons, and valleys. There's not a lot of tillable land here, where the creasing and faulting of the Franciscan geological period left intermittent hunks of serpentine and a ground crust of sandstone and shale. But the soil supports the grasses required for grazing, there's usually rain six months of the year, and the growing season is a long one. And there are creeks. A road map of Marin County shows more creeks in this area than roads—Americano, San Antonio, Chileno, Walker, Novato, Halleck, and Nicasio are the large ones.

Although these ranchlands account for almost one-third of the county's land area, the population comprises less than one-twentieth. This is rural Marin, which has little in common with the populated commuter suburbs of southern Marin.

People here don't carry attaché cases, they don't think a lot about hot-tubs or encounter groups. If they're going to town, they mean Novato or Petaluma, in Sonoma County, not San Francisco. In fact, many ranches in northern Marin have Petaluma addresses and telephone exchanges. Children go to high school in Petaluma. After school, teenagers are more likely to spend the afternoon cleaning stalls or sliding on a tray down a hilly pasture than eating french fries at the local takeout. Their parents, if still awake at 10:00 P.M., might sink into the sofa to watch TV, but seldom drive to town for a movie or a bite to eat.

On the Point Reyes–Petaluma Road, the only odor strong enough to compete with cow manure is cheese. The Marin French Cheese Company has plenty of that. It's the only producer of Camembert cheese west of the Mississippi. Ed Thompson is in his mid-seventies, has pink cheeks and a Norman Rockwell twinkle. He runs the Marin French Cheese Company with his cousin Pierce Thompson and several other family members.

A hundred years ago there were some fifteen cheese makers in this part of Marin. The Thompson company was the only one to survive. Today it's an enormously successful business. The company's Rouge et Noir label Bries and Camemberts are sold all over the West—from Safeways and Luckys to chic gourmet shops. Now the Thompsons are eyeing the New York market. But Ed Thompson still thinks of himself as a country boy. "In the old days," he says, "you didn't tell a rancher what he could do with his land. The old-timers did what they wanted, provided they didn't step on a neighbor's toes. Today you need a permit to do anything. If it's not the Water District, it's the Coastal Commission, the Park Service, the EPA, or Fish and Game." He shakes his head. "It's gone too far." His adopted son, Doug, nods in agreement.

Allen Moore, a tall blond with an easy gait and a floppy mustache, strides toward the front drive of Dexter's Nicasio Valley Arabians, his boots clapping against the cement breeze-way by the stables. Allen used to be a surfer in L.A., then a cowboy in Oregon; now he's a horse breeder. He manages the Arabian horse ranch for George Dexter, who also owns four automobile dealerships in the Bay Area. A four-wheel-drive truck trailing a spotless white horse van pulls up the gravel drive. Allen Moore waves to the new arrival. Everything looks new at Dexter's—the fence posts, the tile-roofed stables, the front paddock with grass so green you look for the sprinkler system. The ranch is small—what is commonly known as a "ranchette" in these parts. "This isn't the sticks anymore," says Allen. "There's all kinds of houses and ranchettes going in around here. In ten or fifteen years it'll be another Beverly Hills. By that time I'll be gone."

Between 1834 and 1838, the governors of Mexico issued seven land grants in this part of Marin County. By far the largest was Rancho Nicasio, 56,807 acres extending north from San Geronimo to Tomales, and east to Rancho Novato. Governor Juan Alvarado had promised the tract to the Coast Miwok Indians, many of whom were homeless after the Mexican government secularized and dismantled Mission San Rafael in 1834. Instead, Alvarado's successor awarded Rancho Nicasio to Pablo de la Guerra and Juan Cooper. Like so many early land grants, this one stayed in the hands of its original owners only briefly. By 1850, most of Rancho Nicasio belonged to Henry Halleck,

Windmill, Hicks Valley

GENTLEMEN FARMERS

It is a familiar story in urbanizing areas throughout the state: intense pressure for conversion of agricultural lands to residential development results in a rise in land values; increasing costs for feed, labor, and equipment; and conflicts between rural and urban uses, make selling out appealing.

There are buyers for 60-acre homesites in Nicasio—call them gentlemen farmers, seekers of rural solitude, or what you will—and they will pay far higher prices than any rancher buying land for ranching would or could. . . .

To ranchers who want to keep on ranching, to suburban dwellers in Marin's rural areas, to lovers of open space wherever it is, that is a pessimistic story. . . .

MARGARET AZEVEDO
INDEPENDENT JOURNAL
MARCH 10, 1979

DROUGHT TAKES TOLL ON LOCAL DAIRIES

Two drought years combined with anti-pollution guidelines are quietly taking their toll of West Marin dairies. Since the beginning of December, eight of Marin County's 72 dairies have shut down—with half the closures in West Marin. . . .

Some 24 Marin County ranches are now hauling water, and another 15 to 20 are expected to be hauling by summer. . . .

POINT REYES LIGHT
JULY 14, 1977

MARIN ANIMAL DISEASES

There aren't too many veterinary problems unique to Marin county. We probably see a higher incidence of disease caused by wet weather than vets in drier places. Red water is fairly common here. It comes from spores that live in the soil. In the winter rains, the spores wash into low-lying places—canyons and bogs. If cows ingest a lot of them, they can die. We probably see more liver flukes here, and a little more pneumonia than Valley vets. Anti-plasmosis, a tick-born parasite that causes anemia, is also more common in Marin. The ticks come from the brush and chaparral on the hills. You won't see the disease again until you get to the Sierra foothills. In general, the weather and grazing advantages of Marin ranchlands far outweigh the problems from associated diseases.

ROBERT FISHER, VETERINARIAN
POINT REYES STATION
APRIL 1980

James Miller, and James Black.

During the Gold Rush, many Yankee lawyers and farmers settled in Marin County. They were followed by Scottish, Irish, and Portuguese dairymen, who started as milkers and later bought ranches from their land-rich, cash-poor predecessors. In the 1870s, a wave of Swiss-Italian immigrants arrived in Marin. As they prospered, they bought ranches of their own and sent for wives and families in Switzerland.

Many of Marin's Swiss-Italian families still work the ranches of their forebears. Mailboxes along Chileno, Hicks, Lucas, and Nicasio valleys bear their names: Morini, Lanatti, Spaletta, La Franchi, Maggetti, Grossi, Respini, Barboni, Dolcini.

Ralph Grossi is the president of the Farm Bureau of Marin County. He is thirty-one years old. With his father, he runs a dairy and cattle ranch on Novato Creek. Grossi graduated from California Polytechnic University with a degree in Dairy Science. He is one of Marin County's most innovative, forward-looking ranchers. The improvements he has made on his own ranch include the installation of the first methane-powered electrical generator in the county. Cow manure is the raw energy source. With Gary Giacomini, Ellen Straus, and several Marin conservationists, he is also developing the Agricultural Land Trust. If it succeeds, the trust will help keep agricultural land in productive use. "The older generation has its own ways of doing things," says Ralph. "It's hard convincing them to try new things. Dairies in Marin County are family-run operations; sometimes the generations clash if the kids want to make changes and the parents won't let go of the reins. Parents and children have to learn to have adult relationships with each other. It isn't easy."

The dairy business is Marin County's largest industry. Milk sales bring some thirty-eight million dollars a year to the county. But ranches in Marin County are small by California standards. They average about eight hundred acres, and herd sizes range from two hundred to four hundred cows, whereas ranches in the San Joaquin Valley average herds of about three thousand. Many of these ranches are owned by large corporations with capital to invest in new equipment and to make the

THREE GENERATIONS

For as long as he can remember, Al [Poncia] had always planned to join the family dairy business, begun by his late grandfather, Angelo, in 1901 and carried on by his father, Alfred, who died in 1977.

"I never thought I'd be anything else," he says. "I loved being a kid on the ranch . . . the rafts on the creek, the treehouses . . . the hiking . . . I knew every rock on the place. . . ."

He cherishes the unique experiences of country life, "spring on the duck pond, a special sunrise, having a picnic on the creek, hearing a meteorite explode in the quiet of dawn, watching things grow."

Even the day-to-day chores—like replacing a broken gate—have charm for him. "I love the sense of accomplishment, knowing I did it myself."

PAT ANGLE
INDEPENDENT JOURNAL
SEPTEMBER 18, 1980

Union District School, Marshall-Petaluma Road

improvements often required by government agencies. In 1974, when the Regional Water Quality Control Board insisted ranches eliminate manure runoff into creeks and bay waters, the small ranches of northern and West Marin were hit hard. Conforming to code often required building "free-stall" barns and manure pits for dumping waste. Changes were expensive. Some ranches went out of business; others are still in the process of making improvements.

Because there are so many government agencies whose policies affect ranchers, you hear a lot of grumbling about "big government" in rural Marin. The California Coastal Commission, the National Park Service, the Bay Area Conservation and Development Commission are just a few of the agencies whose guidelines affect many ranchers.

Like most family businesses, Marin ranches suffer when there are no family members to take over from the preceding generation. Female children are not usually considered candidates, and sometimes sons aren't interested in working the ranch. Says Merv Zimmerman, who has a dairy in Marshall: "One of my sons works at a tile center in Santa Rosa. He saw how hard his daddy worked—seven days a week, with no time off to help with 4-H or take ski trips, and he didn't want that kind of life."

Life on a dairy ranch isn't easy. Cows are milked twice a day—from 2:00 A.M. to 6:30 A.M., and again from 1:00 P.M. to 6:00 P.M. Between milkings, stalls have to be cleaned, the dairy washed down, cows fed their silage and alfalfa rations. Dairy cows calve year 'round, so fertility and pregnancy tests must be given, pregnant cows checked for complications, new calves fed and examined. Most dairymen keep a close watch on their herd, calling a veterinarian only if they have a problem they can't handle. When they do need a vet, the vet comes to them. A Holstein with pneumonia or a quarter horse with an abscessed knee is hard to transport.

Robert Fisher, D.V.M., has a "large animal" practice in Point Reyes Station. His clients include many of Marin's horse, cattle, and dairy ranchers. Robert and his partners "train" their clients when to call and what cases are urgent. A cow with a prolapsed uterus needs immediate attention. A sterility test can wait until morning.

A cow to whom antibiotics have been given has to be kept

DAYS OF THE DONS

"Sometimes it is true, it makes me sad to think of all the Rancho being gone. As a boy I used to ride, chasing the cattle, climbing the steep mountain sides followed by our vaqueros. . . . and how wild it was then and so beautiful—so beautiful!"

Quoted by HELEN BINGHAM
IN TAMAL LAND (1906)

A MIWOK "SWEATHOUSE"

The aborigines' knowledge of the proper treatment of disease was very limited. Roots and herbs were sometimes used as remedies but the "sweathouse" (temescal) was the principal reliance in desperate cases. One of these sweathouses was found on the Nicasio Rancheria, just over the Olompali Mountains.

It consisted of a large circular excavation, covered with a roof of boughs, plastered with mud, having a hole on one side for an entrance, another in the roof to serve as a chimney.

A fire having been lit in the center, the sick were placed there to undergo a sweat bath for many hours, to be succeeded by a plunge in the ice-cold waters of a neighboring stream.

This treatment was their cure-all, and whether it killed or relieved the patient depended upon the nature of his disease and his constitution.

HELEN BINGHAM
IN TAMAL LAND (1906)

from the rest of the herd or clearly marked so that it won't be milked until treatment is completed. Dairies store their milk in large, stainless-steel holding tanks. Each day, before the milk is transferred to the tank truck, the driver tests the milk for bacteria, drugs, and other contaminants. Most Marin dairies are members of the Petaluma Creamery Cooperative, which sells and delivers to large dairy distributors, like Berkeley Farms, Lucky Stores, Knudsen, and Safeway's Lucerne. If undetected, contaminated milk from one cow can ruin the distributor's entire output. So ranchers are scrupulously careful.

Most ranchers employ at least two milking hands. Ranchers and milkers agree that it's a tough job. The odd hours are part of the problem. So are the personality clashes. Ranch hands live in bachelor quarters or dorms. When hands don't get along, the turnover, usually about six months to a year and a half, is even higher.

Today, many Marin ranch hands are Mexican. Ranchers are required to see "green cards," or work permits, before employing Mexican laborers. Inspectors can make trouble for the employee without a green card and the rancher who employs him. A milker's wages are usually pretty low, but with room and board paid for, some hands can save six or seven hundred dollars a month. Many Mexicans send for their families in Mexico when they've saved enough. Others go home.

It's a tradition in the dairy business that the newest immigrant arrivals start as milkers and work up. But with land values skyrocketing in the county, it's no longer easy for anyone to "buy in." And there's more to a dairy than just owning the land and a herd of cows. You also need a "quota," which determines how much milk you can sell. Without a quota, you can't sell milk. When milk surpluses are high, as they have been recently, quotas are hard to get.

When the early dairymen began ranching in Marin County, their herds were primarily Jersey cows, shipped from the East Coast. Jersey milk is very rich, with high butterfat content. Today's marketplace demands thinner, low-fat milk. Most dairies still have a few Jerseys, but Holsteins predominate.

Beef cattle are less expensive to maintain than milkers. They require fewer hands—one hand per three hundred head is the rule of thumb. Herefords are the choice of Marin

The "Running Fence," 1976

CHRISTO'S FENCE

Christo's Running Fence is running again, in the Maysles brothers' film now being shown in San Francisco and elsewhere. . . .

The ranchers across whose land the Fence had run, the long-haired kids who'd built it, and the short-haired engineers who'd shown them how, were all crowded into the little old schoolhouse. They greeted themselves and their friends on the screen with unabashed pleasure and hooted at any hapless soul who sounded the least bit pompous or overblown. They cheered Christo whenever he appeared.

Say what you will about the man, no showman on earth could have faked the affection that flowed out to him from that crowd that afternoon, and from him back to them. It was evident they shared a joyous memory.

MARGARET AZEVEDO
INDEPENDENT JOURNAL
MARCH 21, 1978

ranchers. More agile and mobile than dairy cows, beef cattle can graze on slopes too steep and hazardous for Holsteins. Most graze year 'round on the range, an advantage not shared by San Joaquin Valley ranchers, who run "dry lot," pastureless operations.

The Dolcini family is one of the largest Swiss-Italian clans in Marin County. With over three hundred family members in the area, the family owns some twelve thousand acres in Marin County, making them Marin's largest landholders.

The family's Marin roots date back to the 1860s, when Peter Dolcini, a dairyman from Lake Lugano, Switzerland, arrived in Marin County. Peter married the daughter of Charles Martin, a Swiss dairyman and Marin landowner himself.

Susan Dolcini is Peter's great-great-grandchild. Her father, Arnold, was a dairyman and cattle rancher, but his real love was horse breeding. When Arnold died two years ago, Susan, who knew more about quarter horses than did her older sister and three older brothers, took over many of her father's responsibilities. Someday she would like to have a horse ranch of her own, but she doesn't expect it will be the family ranch. "No matter how you work it out," she says philosophically, "it's always gonna be the males who dominate."

Susan wasn't yet born when her father started breeding horses, but she's heard the story enough times to remember it well. "In the fifties, my dad bought a mare named Teresa Tivio in Sacramento. He paid five hundred dollars for Tess, and everybody laughed. That was a lot of money. But Dad liked her breeding, and it turned out she was a really good horse. She's produced over twenty registered quarter horses and six are national champions."

The Dolcinis' horses aren't just for show. Several are used in the cattle operation, managed by Susan's oldest brother, Steve. "I like the beef business," says Steve. "You're not tied down all the time. You don't have to milk twice a day and you can set your own pace. But there are always problems."

One of the problems is the fluctuating price of beef. Milk prices are uniform, based on a national formula that takes feed and other production costs into account. But beef prices change constantly.

"You've got to be thrifty in the beef business," says Steve,

INVENTORIES OF
MARIN LIVESTOCK & POULTRY

ITEM	Jan. 1, 1980
Cattle & Calves	37,000
All Dairy Cows & Heifers that have calved	12,600
Beef Cattle & Heifers that have calved	6,500
Calves	19,100
Stock Sheep & Lambs	10,500
Hogs	200
Poultry	113,200

COUNTY OF MARIN
ANNUAL LIVESTOCK AND AGRICULTURAL
CROP REPORT

Old fence, Middle Road

"because you never know what will happen to the price from year to year."

All of Arnold Dolcini's children seem to have inherited the Dolcini love for ranching and for Marin County. "We're carrying on my father's dream," says Susan. "I sleep in the room where my father slept as a baby. I'm walking in his footsteps. Living here is a neat feeling. It's peaceful, and you have pride in your land and your animals. I wouldn't develop myself if I stayed on the ranch all my life. You get too isolated. But I'll come back. There'll always be a place for me here."

Most of Marin's dairy and cattle ranchers hope there will always be places for their kids to come back to. If the Agricultural Land Trust is successfully established, some will sell or donate their development easements to the trust. This will insure that their land stays agricultural and will reduce costly inheritance taxes by decreasing land values. Others hope increased milk and beef prices will simply make their operations more profitable.

In the meantime, the future of pastoral Marin is still uncertain. A-60 zoning has not stopped residential development entirely. There are many newcomers who can afford to buy sixty-acre ranchettes, which, while making attractive homes and estates, usually take agricultural land out of production.

Ralph Grossi is optimistic about the future of rural Marin. "Those of us who stay in the dairy business will be in a good position in the years to come. We're sixty minutes from San Francisco and a major consumer market. We have some of the best native pastures in the state. If a lot of productive ranchland is eaten up by urban sprawl, it would be a terrible waste. We're doing the best we can do to be sure that doesn't happen."

Corral, Marshall-Petaluma Road

Reservoir, Nicasio Valley

Ranchlands

Morelli Ranch, Red Hill Road

Dairy barns, Middle Road

Sheep ranch near Marsh Road

Cattle ranch, Nicasio Road

Saint Mary's Catholic Church, Nicasio

NICASIO SCHOOL.

Nicasio School

Milking barns, Robert Dolcini Ranch

JOHN LUND

Mailboxes, Hicks Valley Road

Lincoln District School, Hicks Valley Road

Calf inoculation, Robert Dolcini Ranch

Winter rain, Chileno Valley Road

Pasture, Marshall-Petaluma Road

Americano Creek

M***ARIN northwest***

Pig farm, Whitaker Bluff Road

Abandoned ranch, Middle Road

Cattle gate, Whitaker Bluff Road

Part 3

Fishing pier, Fort Baker

BAY SHORES: Inside the Golden Gate

Chapter 6 _____ Waterside Worlds, South

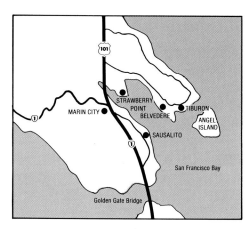

Sausalito
Marin City
The Tiburon Peninsula
(Strawberry Point, Belvedere, Tiburon)
Angel Island

Sausalito

7:00 A.M. The sun reaches over Angel Island and breaks the waters of Richardson Bay into a thousand flashing mirrors. The wind offers the sun a morning greeting, lifting plumes of spray into the air and rocking the houseboats at Sausalito's Gate 5. A bearded man in black rubber boots emerges from the cabin of a brown-shingled barge. He scratches the small tiger cat sleeping in the petunia barrel on the deck, then waters the tomato plants growing in the dinghy tied to his boat.

On Bridgeway, a garbage truck rumbles slowly along the waterfront, past Ondine's Restaurant, the Upstart Crow Bookstore, and the Cafe Triesté. Its metal jaws gulp down a breakfast of crab shells, coffee grounds, and cardboard boxes.

In the Sausalito hills, bright bougainvillea vines and eucalyptus trees tremble in the breeze. Coffee mug in hand, a groggy commuter stands on a hillside deck, gazing across the rippling water of Richardson Bay.

At 9:00 A.M., the first ferryload of San Francisco tourists will walk down the gangplank at El Portal and begin their inspection of Sausalito's waterfront shops and restaurants. For many travelers, Sausalito will be the only place they visit in Marin. Judging by the smiles, sunburns, and packages they carry back with them on the afternoon ferry, they are well pleased.

Marin County is a little like a Rorschach test. Its varied and dramatic landscapes invite associations with other, often exotic places. The rugged coastal bluffs of Point Reyes remind some of northern Scotland. The hot, brown hills of interior Marin become the sun-scorched stretches of southern Italy. And Sausalito, Marin's southernmost town, is invariably compared to the Mediterranean—the Côte d'Azur, the French Riviera.

In 1775, when the first Europeans entered San Francisco Bay

Fishing boat off Sausalito

Sunday painter, Sausalito

SAUSALITO'S CHARMS

There is something in the spirit of this hillside gardening, this planting of sweet blossoms for the public at large, that is very appealing in these days of monopolistic greed, when everything that is worthwhile has a fence around it. Thus it is refreshing to find a little spot in this dollar-mad America where the citizens disinterestedly beautify the public streets for the enjoyment of each passer-by.

HELEN BINGHAM
IN TAMAL LAND (1906)

on the ship *San Carlos,* they were enchanted by the sheltered cove they found inside the Golden Gate. The Spanish crew called it Saucelito, for the "little willows" growing by her creeks and springs. Although the *San Carlos* moved quickly on to a new anchorage at Angel Island, other vessels would continue to moor in Sausalito.

Captain William Richardson, the first white man to live and work in Marin County, supplied many of these vessels with water from Sausalito's natural springs. His wharf at Shelter Cove was the maritime center of early Marin, his adobe home a social center.

During the Gold Rush, Richardson's fortunes dwindled, but Sausalito flourished. Many ships' captains preferred docking in Sausalito rather than San Francisco, where their crews were more likely to jump ship and head for the gold country. British mariners were particularly fond of Sausalito; when Sausalito's first subdivision was created in the 1860s, they built homes in the hills above the waterfront. Here they could watch the sidewheeler *Princess* make her newly scheduled daily runs between San Francisco and Sausalito.

The year 1874 was an important one for the town because the North Pacific Coast Railroad chose Sausalito as the terminus for its narrow-gauge line to West Marin. Linked to ferry service, the railroad, later to become the North Shore, then the Northwestern Pacific, lured many of San Francisco's new monied gentry to the Sausalito hills, where they hoped, perhaps, that the cultivated manners of the British colony already established there would rub off. Hotels and summer villas, like Sea Point, the home of William Randolph Hearst in the 1890s, dotted the hills. Some called the hills, with their tropical, leisurely ambience, the "banana belt."

Bustling with rail and maritime traffic, Sausalito's waterfront became the "garlic belt." Italian and Portuguese settlers netted salmon, bass, herring, and shrimp in the bay, or waited on tables at hotels and restaurants. The town's thriving saloons and gambling halls were given a boost in the 1890s, when San Francisco placed a ban on track gambling. Gamblers headed across the Golden Gate for Sausalito. The city fathers welcomed the business, but not the Sausalito Women's Club, formed in 1913 to clean up the town.

Prohibition dealt a blow to the newly reformed Sausalito.

ON FINE SUNDAY MORNINGS

**On fine Sunday mornings he would gather
friends together for—often somewhat
perilous—jaunts on the *Perfidia*, Yanko
[Jean Varda] being a stubbornly proud sailor
who would permit no motor aboard his boat,
so that we were often becalmed or carried
away by strong tides. Yet *Perfidia* was the
bravest boat on the Bay, with eyes on the
prow, a broad band of vivid red below the
gunwales, and a honey-colored lateen sail.
There was room aboard for at least a dozen
passengers, often including such notable
beauties as Anne Ryan, Henrietta DiSuvero,
Clare Wiles, and Ruth Costello, dressed in
their brightest and supplied with loaves and
cold chicken and gallons of wine. Seeing this
craft gliding in full sail by the wooded cliffs
of Belvedere, it was impossible to believe
that this was the United States and not the
islands of Greece.**

ALAN WATTS
IN MY OWN WAY (1972)

Ferryboat VALLEJO, Gate 5, Sausalito

Speakeasies thrived. From the old Silva Mansion, Baby Face Nelson managed a bootlegging operation, smuggling Canadian whiskey from West Marin to San Francisco. Some say that Pretty Boy Floyd tended bar at the Valhalla, Marin's oldest continuously operated saloon, now owned by a former San Francisco "madam" and Sausalito mayor, Sally Stanford. "Nice" people stayed away from Sausalito, or its downtown area, anyway.

In 1941, four years after the opening of the Golden Gate Bridge, Sausalito lost its trains and ferries. (But in 1970, the Golden Gate Bridge, Highway and Transit District restored ferry service.) The waterfront railyards became the site of a booming shipyard in World War II. At the request of the U.S. Maritime Commission, the Bechtel Corporation erected Marin Shipyards, on 202 acres of the waterfront. During the three years of its existence, the shipyard produced ninety-three vessels, including fourteen Liberty ships and sixty-two tankers. "Marinship" employed some twenty thousand people—more women than any other West Coast yard and, incidentally, sixty percent of the San Francisco Symphony Orchestra.

In the 1960s, the old piers at Marinship provided rent-free homesites for a community of writers, artists, and families attracted to Sausalito's waterfront. Rescuing abandoned skiffs, tugboats, even antiaircraft-balloon barges from Richardson Bay, the newcomers developed a unique lifestyle. Houseboat living was casual, communal, caring, and inexpensive. Artist Piro Caro made his home on the old ferry *Issaquah.* Philosopher Alan Watts and painter Jean Varda rehabilitated the *Vallejo,* a double-ended ferry that once ran between San Francisco and Mare Island in San Pablo Bay. Aldous and Laura Huxley, Allen Ginsberg, Fritz Perls, and Duke Ellington were among those who participated in public events on the *Vallejo,* which is now the home of the Alan Watts Society for Comparative Philosophy.

Today there are over three hundred houseboats on Sausalito's waterfront. But life is not as relaxed and live-and-let-live as it was once. For more than a decade, houseboaters have fought attempts by real-estate developers to convert the waterfront into expensive berth sites and private marinas. Houseboats are required to conform to county utility and housing codes, and most have been forced to tie up to perma-

Houseboat, Sausalito

KEROUAC'S MARIN CITY

Mill City, where Remi lived, was a collection of shacks in a valley, housing-project shacks built for Navy Yard workers during the war; it was in a canyon, and a deep one, treed profusely on all slopes. There were special stores and barber shops and tailor shops for the people of the project. It was, so they say, the only community in America where whites and Negroes lived together voluntarily; and that was so, and so wild and joyous a place I've never seen since.

JACK KEROUAC
ON THE ROAD (1955)

nent piers. Many old-timers and small-boat owners have left, tired of fighting developers, county codes, and high rents. Professionals, commuters, and more affluent Marinites have taken their place. Elaborately designed suburban-style houses now float near teepee-roofed barges, remodeled cabooses, geodesic domes.

Despite the changes in Sausalito, many houseboaters are unwilling to abandon their floating community. Says one resident, quoted in *Houseboat*, by Ben Dennis and Betsy Case: "I'll stay on the water always. Its moods constantly change. The fog lifts. The tides roll in."

Marin City

Marin City is the only community in Marin where black residents easily outnumber whites. Tucked between Sausalito on the south and Tamalpais Valley on the northwest, it was a 350-acre tract of dairy and marshland until 1942, when Marinship opened in Sausalito. Some six thousand of the shipyard's twenty thousand workers lived in temporary housing constructed at Marin City. About half of the residents were black; they had come to Marin from the Deep South and the Midwest.

The closing of Marinship after World War II hit black workers hardest. They were unemployed and isolated in an upper-middle-class, white county with very little industry, whose residential communities were racially restrictive. Many blacks stayed on in Marin City's wartime housing.

In 1956 the United States Housing Authority unveiled a master plan for Marin City. Called a "milestone" in urban redevelopment, the project's blueprints promised a better life for Marin City residents. In addition to apartments, co-ops, and private homes, the plan called for a "downtown" that would contain schools, recreational facilities, a light industrial park, and a business district.

As an incentive to the California Development Company, Marin County sold the firm 167 acres of valuable Marin City ridgeland property for far less than its open-market value. In return, the developer would also build the "downtown" of what was considered a socially and economically marginal community. Today there is still no "downtown" in Marin City. When the housing was completed, the construction

THE FLEA MARKET

"I dearly love the flea market," François says, "it's a real people's market. They come down from the hills and trade; they set their own prices, it fights inflation. If the big markets try to take over, I'd fight it. I'm upset because a lot of my friends are being pushed out of Marin; if you can't foot the bill you have to go. People who don't have 'it' think they can buy 'it' in Marin. They come here and whatever the rents are, they're willing to pay them. Why should the dollar determine who lives here and who doesn't?"

ELIZABETH STEWART
"LIVING ON LESS"
PACIFIC SUN, 1980

PARADISE-ON-THE-FERRY

The ferry landings were gathering spots for city-bound residents of Marin and Marin-bound day employees. Housemaids and merchants, bookkeepers and brokers, deliverymen and dowagers, coming and going across the bay at all hours of the day and even late into the night. They developed many friendly ties with each other on the ferries. This strengthened the sense of community in Marin. The "hill people" from the Tamalpais communities and the "flatland people" from San Rafael and the lowland communities beside the bay rubbed shoulders on the ferries and knew themselves to be all Marinites.

DR. EVELYN MORRIS RADFORD
THE BRIDGE AND THE BUILDING (1973)

came to an end for almost twenty years.

Years later, the developer built on the land he had acquired in 1960. Completed in the 1970s, town houses and condominiums at Richardson Highlands sold at prices few Marin City residents could afford—from $170,000 to $240,000.

Many of Marin City's residents are angry. They call themselves the county's forgotten "stepchildren." Recently, black leaders in the community formed the Community Development Corporation to acquire new property, including ten and a half acres, now used by the Marin City Flea Market, for development of the promised downtown and commercial area. An oak table or an antique faucet is fine, say some, but it's not a loaf of bread, a gallon of milk, a place to work or to own a business.

Community leader Bettie Hodges speaks for many of Marin City's disenfranchised. "We've chosen to live here," she told a reporter recently, "because it's a community, a family, and we're interested in seeing that continue. Marin City has a little over five hundred families. It's a microcosm of problems that exist in the cities. Here, these problems seem manageable. If poor people can gain control of their community, they can survive."

The Tiburon Peninsula

There are a few people in Marin who never go *in* the water, but almost everybody likes to *look* at the water. With seventeen miles of continuous shoreline, the Tiburon Peninsula is one of the most popular residential communities in the county. Richardson Bay laps against the southern flanks of the hump-backed peninsula, and San Francisco Bay borders its northern shores. Whether walking the dog on Strawberry Point, sipping piña coladas on a Belvedere deck, or playing Monopoly in a Tiburon town house, residents usually have one eye on the water. The bay waters beckoned the Coast Miwok Indians over one thousand years ago and welcomed John Reed in 1834. Reed's land grant, Corte de Madera del Presidio, included all of the peninsula, running west to Mill Valley and north to Larkspur.

Although Mexican longhorns no longer graze on the grassy *potreros* of Tiburon, Belvedere, or Strawberry, and the Indians' shoreline villages are gone, the peninsula continues to attract

A CALL TO PROTECT STRAWBERRY SEALS

The Strawberry Spit is a significant habitat for harbor seals in San Francisco Bay and should be preserved as a marine mammal sanctuary, a scientific study for the federal government has recommended. . . .

"The critical need is to minimize disturbance at major haul-out sites, particularly on Strawberry Spit in northwestern San Francisco Bay, and to provide for the long-term protection and maintenance of these sites.

"If this is accomplished, harbor seals could continue to coexist indefinitely with man in this highly industrialized and urbanized environment."

INDEPENDENT JOURNAL
FEBRUARY 25, 1980

BELVEDERE SOCIETY

When Belvedere dreamed this dream of being the Tuxedo of the Pacific slope, it built some stout iron gates, which divided the island proper from the strip of land which leads up to its sacred precincts, and those gates were provided with patent fastenings and duly barred against the unprivileged non-resident, unless, indeed, he came to call. . . . Belvedere acquired a certain importance in the way of wickedness. It was known, especially in San Rafael, as "fast". . . . So Belvedere had its cliques and its wheels within wheels, and although it could not be called fashionable it was not without its social distractions.

SAN FRANCISCO EXAMINER
JULY 21, 1895

newcomers. "I love living so close to the water," says one resident. "It's like being on vacation all year 'round. It's soothing and so totally luxurious."

Strawberry Point

In the 1970s, construction began on eighty-three luxury homes on Strawberry Point, which juts out into Richardson Bay. Before they were completed, thirty percent of the houses had been purchased by Iranians and Saudi Arabians from the oil-rich Middle East. Before their arrival, the Golden Gate Baptist Theological Seminary had had much of the mile-long peninsula to itself. If Moslem suburbanites seem a strange contrast to six hundred Baptist seminarians, consider one of Strawberry's earliest settlers. His name was Benjamin Lyford. After moving to California from the East, he opened a medical practice in San Francisco, astonished locals with his lifelike and long-lasting embalming techniques, and married Hilarita Reed. Hilarita inherited a large portion of the Tiburon Peninsula, including Strawberry, from her father, John Reed. The marriage permitted Lyford to give up his medical practice and embark on a career that established him as one of Marin's most inventive and eccentric entrepreneurs.

In 1876, the Lyfords built a wood-frame Victorian home on Strawberry Point and began the operation of the Eagle Dairy. Lyford claimed that kindness was the key to his cows' high milk production; he treated his Jerseys kindly, and they returned the favor. A fanatic on matters of hygiene, Lyford introduced pasteurization to local ranchers. He also whitewashed the ties on the North Pacific Coast Railroad, where it ran behind his house. Today Lyford's Victorian house still stands, but not on Strawberry. In 1957, the National Audubon Society moved the house across Richardson Bay to Tiburon. It is now headquarters for the nine-hundred-acre Richardson Bay Wildlife Sanctuary.

Belvedere

Think of Belvedere as a long green ocean liner moored to Tiburon's southeastern shore by two causeways, one at the stern, one amidships. High above the water, on the ship's prow, is the imposing portico of the old Blanding mansion. Other large houses, wedged into the cliffs on both sides of the

Main Street, Tiburon, circa 1880

ARKVILLE

In the inlet and over in the haven of Belvedere opposite, a colony of house-boats, calling themselves, I believe, "Arkville," lies at anchor all through the summer months. Some are simply a couple of rooms built upon the hull of an old scow, but others are furnished with the greatest comfort: large wicker chairs upon their verandas, dainty blue curtains at their windows, comfortable beds inside, and at night strings of Venetian lanterns lighted round their decks. Their inmates seem to live in bathing suits, diving from the porches, paddling about in dories or canoes, living upon the fish they catch, and leading a sort of semi-aquatic existence generally.

ERNEST PEIXOTTO
ROMANTIC CALIFORNIA (1910)

SOUTHERN PACIFIC BUILDS A TOWN WITHIN A TOWN

Southern Pacific will unveil detailed plans for the development of its 38 acres in downtown Tiburon at 9 A.M. Jan. 26 in the Del Mar School music room.

The Town Council has already approved the general master plan for the railroad's development. It includes 164 condominiums and up to 68,500 square feet of retail and office space. The railroad also proposes renovations to the existing freshwater marsh, an open shoreline park, improved streets and drainage and three tennis courts.

INDEPENDENT JOURNAL
JANUARY 6, 1980

island, are the private staterooms, with portholes overlooking Belvedere Cove, Belvedere Lagoon, and Richardson Bay. Dining, dancing, and recreation take place on the lower decks, at the San Francisco and Corinthian Yacht Clubs. No shuffleboard here, but plenty of Coppertone, Cabernet, and mahogany. Passengers like the beauty and privacy this waterside life provides. Don't wander aboard their ship uninvited. You may be politely but firmly escorted down the gangplank.

Belvedere has all the charms of island life without the inconveniences. Whether by car or by the Tiburon ferry, the commute to San Francisco is easy, and San Francisco Bay is the most popular recreational boating area in Northern California.

In 1890, Thomas B. Valentine recognized Belvedere's unique advantages when he founded the Belvedere Land Company and sold homesites on the island. At that time Belvedere was even more private, connected to Tiburon by only one natural causeway at the northwestern end.

One attraction in the 1880s and '90s was Belvedere Cove, where the county's first houseboat community gained a reputation for lavish entertaining and a spirited sporting life. The summer colony was sometimes called Arkville. Its vessels were arks—long, flat-bottomed boats that could remain upright if low tide left parts of the cove exposed. Early arks were of simple design and belonged to local fishermen or sporting clubs. Later models were elaborate. The *Nautilus* was fashioned from four retired San Francisco streetcars. The *California* boasted an eighteen-foot social hall and six staterooms.

"Ark-hopping" was a favorite sport of San Francisco bachelors, who rowed from boat to boat, paying housecalls and often staying for meals or a party. Local merchants supplied ark owners with food and drink, delivered in rowboats from the shore. San Francisco commuters went to work on the *Favorite,* a private steam launch that picked them up each morning and dropped them off at their arks every afternoon.

"There is an indescribable charm about the life," wrote a reporter for an English magazine, *The Strand,* in 1899. "One has the pleasures of boating combined with the 'comforts of home'; baths are at one's very threshold and fish are caught and cooked while you wait. The scenery is varied by the swinging of the ark as it turns four times a day with the tide."

Old Saint Hilary's, Tiburon

WHEN THEY PAINTED THE TOWN

Over the weekend of September 24 and 25, 1955, more than 100 volunteers swarmed Main Street [Tiburon] with paint brushes and rollers in hand. The volunteer crews included Tiburon and Belvedere residents, teachers, railroad men, teams of teenagers, firemen, sailors and civilian workers from the Tiburon Naval Net Depot, and even a few professional painters (the project had the approval of the painters' union). Boy Scouts helped to plant flowers in 18 redwood boxes along the sidewalks.

Main Street had been the shopping center for the entire area ever since the railroad began operating, and thereby fostered a town, in 1884. By the mid-1950s, the street was outgrown, its storefronts were weathered, and basic business was shifting away from the waterfront. The last grocery, Beyries', closed in early September. . . .

LOUISE TEATHER
ARK
SEPTEMBER 24, 1975

After the Depression, many of the arks were destroyed. When Belvedere Lagoon, their winter home, was partially filled in the 1950s, a handful of arks were hauled onto Tiburon's Main Street. Painted and restored, a few of the surviving crafts of Arkville help make "Ark Row" one of the most attractive shopping areas in Tiburon.

In 1890, travelers could only get to Tiburon Point via Belvedere. An extension of Tiburon Boulevard now makes the journey more direct. Most Belvedere residents are glad to be bypassed. What some call "the moat mentality," others term "the Garbo syndrome"—"I vant to be alone."

Tiburon

From the wide decks of Main Street's bayside restaurants, with the skyline of San Francisco as a distant background, visitors watch small ferries, framed by blue water and an even bluer sky, chugging across Raccoon Strait from Angel Island. Lured by the scent of crab Louis and eggs Benedict, the seagulls at Sam's and The Dock pace the railings, then descend, in a flurry of feathers, on empty tables. At the Corinthian Yacht Club, skippers snap orders as they guide their boats slowly from the harbor.

In this waterside paradise, it's hard to believe that Tiburon was once a working-class town. But a hundred years ago the Tiburon Peninsula was an industrial seaport with cod fisheries and powder companies. Belvedere Cove was a maritime "crematory," where retired ships were salvaged and burned. San Francisco and North Pacific Railroad trains clanged through the town after meeting the ferries at Tiburon Point. Cows grazed on the hills where houses stand today. The bay waters were clean, alive with shrimp, crab, oyster beds, and waterfowl. But that was when San Francisco Bay, free of landfill, was one-third larger than it is today.

Tiburon was never as fashionable as neighboring Belvedere. But in 1886, Benjamin Lyford announced the opening of a new town and health resort on Tiburon Point. Hygeia, named for the Greek goddess of health, was to be a "center of education, science, art, and an abode where there should be contentment, longevity and a happy, healthy life."

Tiburon Point, with its mild climate and refreshing bay breezes, was far from San Francisco's "noxious gases," which,

Lyford House, Tiburon

MARVELOUS HYGEIA

Of this marvelous spot, which even now events are shaping to become the most far-famed health resort the world has known, of its matchless combination of location, climate, water facilities, freedom from fogs, noxious vapors, and in a word, total immunity from all those elements which retard growth and ultimately destroy life, much has been written, but its true story and the story of the almost supernatural foresight which seems to have guided him who has been foremost in bringing its advantages, its unequaled climatic conditions before the world is yet to be told.

SALES PROSPECTUS
LYFORD'S HYGEIA
(1895)

said Lyford's brochure, "are the primal cause of the great mortality in centers of dense population." Surely the words of an embalmer can be trusted on these matters.

Although San Franciscans were intrigued with Hygeia, Tiburon was still somewhat inaccessible, even with the newly arrived railroad and ferry terminal. Others may have been put off by Lyford's restrictions (not always enforced) on gambling, dancing, drinking, and "anything contrary to good morals."

Fifteen years ago, medical historian Ilza Veith bought Tiburon property that, she discovered, had once been listed as "Parcel 13, Lyford's Hygeia." Although 13 was her family's lucky number and she'd enjoyed a life of "seemingly good health," Veith became seriously ill shortly after she moved in.

Is she bitter? No. But her subsequent studies of Dr. Lyford's Hygeia did not convince her of the doctor's seriousness. "It is disappointing to realize," she writes in the *Journal of Western Medicine* (November 1977), "that much of it was pure pretension. . . . Lyford's Hygeia actually was a well-conceived plan for a successful real-estate venture."

Today not all Marin residents live on the "higher plane of existence" Dr. Lyford wished to cultivate. But most think Tiburon is a great place to live. Many would number themselves among those "hundreds, weary with the carking cares of city life, who look forward to a residence on this spot as an epoch of their lives . . . "

Angel Island

Angel Island has secrets she will never tell. She has hosted Coast Miwok Indians, Spanish explorers, Russian otter hunters, American soldiers, and many others. Today she keeps her own company in the cold waters of San Francisco Bay. The island is a state park, 740 acres crossed with miles of hiking and cycling trails.

In the 1840s, Angel Island belonged to Antonio Osio, who grazed his cattle on the island's *potreros* and cut timber for the presidio at Yerba Buena. Duelists sailed to her shores from San Francisco and Marin, settling their disputes with loaded pistols. In 1853, the United States government wrested the island from Osio. Her hills and coves, so close to the entrance of San Francisco Bay, were ideal for Civil War gun emplacements and a military garrison.

For more than a century the United States Army and Angel Island maintained an unusual relationship. During the Spanish-American War, American troops returning from the Philippines were quarantined on her shores at the U.S. Public Health Station. During World War II, more than ten thousand troops waited on Angel Island before they were shipped overseas.

Isla de los Angeles was the name given the island by the grateful crew of the Spanish ship *San Carlos*. In 1775 they anchored in Ayala Cove for twenty-five days. But for thousands of Chinese immigrants interned on the island before entering the United States, she was the "Ellis Island of the West." Nor is the island remembered fondly by the German and Italian aliens detained there during World War II.

In 1955, Marin's Caroline Livermore spearheaded an effort to preserve Angel Island for public use. Fifteen years later her efforts were rewarded—the island was declared a state park and national landmark. One developer had proposed converting the island into a Disney-style amusement park.

There are no more elk, bears, or cattle on Angel Island. But there are plenty of deer and lots of ground squirrels. Coastal chaparral is slowly growing over the old Nike missile site constructed in the 1950s. At sunset, visitors must depart, heading back on the last ferry runs to Tiburon and San Francisco. The island is left in solitude. The deer are free to wander as they please.

Angel Island

"WOOD ISLAND"

Having collected nearly all the hides that were to be procured, we began our preparations for taking in a supply of wood and water, for both of which San Francisco is the best place on the coast. A small island, situated about two leagues from the anchorage, called by us "Wood Island," and by the Spaniards "Isla de los Angelos," was covered with trees to the water's edge; and to this, two of our crew, who were Kennebec men, and could handle an axe like a plaything, were sent every morning to cut wood, with two boys to pile it up for them.

RICHARD HENRY DANA, JR.
TWO YEARS BEFORE THE MAST (1846)

THIS PLACE

This place is called an island of immortals, When, in fact, this mountain wilderness is a prison. . . .

**I, a seven foot man, am ashamed I cannot
    extend myself.
Curled up in an enclosure, my movements
    are dictated by others.
Enduring a hundred humiliations, I can only
    cry in vain.
This person's tears fall, but what can the blue
    heavens do?**

INSCRIPTION FROM A WALL AT ANGEL ISLAND IMMIGRATION STATION
ISLAND: POETRY AND HISTORY OF CHINESE IMMIGRANTS ON ANGEL ISLAND 1910–1940
HIM MARK LAI, GENNY LIM, JUDY YUNG (1980)

Fog over Wolfback Ridge

SAUSALITO

Bridgeway

Richardson Street *Jack London House, "Old Town"*

Viña del Mar Plaza, Sausalito

Reflection, Sausalito

Waterside view, Sausalito

Waterfront restaurant, Sausalito

Corinthian Island, Belvedere Cove

TIBURON

Weekend brunch

Tiburon docks

Main Street

Angel Island Ferry, Tiburon

Angel Island, from Elephant Rock, Tiburon

Chapter 7 ———————— Waterside Worlds, North

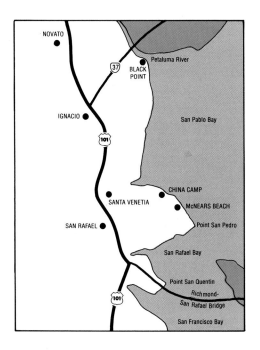

Point San Quentin

In 1850, when an enterprising Yankee bought Rancho Punta de Quentin from its owner, Juan Cooper, he had ambitious plans for the San Quentin Peninsula. On the foggy point protruding into San Francisco Bay, Benjamin Buckelew dreamed of building "Marin City," stepdaughter of "California City," the metropolis he had hoped to create on Tiburon. Two years later, Buckelew was glad to sell off twenty acres of the property to the State of California . . . for a prison.

The first San Quentin prison was not in a building but a brig—the *Waban*, moored off the point from 1852 to 1854. A permanent prison was completed in 1854; San Quentin has operated continuously ever since. Today the prison occupies 440 acres. Three thousand men are housed in four "mainline" cellblocks and one maximum-security "locked" block.

Conditions today have improved since the 1860s, when guards were as tattered as the prisoners, and floggings were routine. In 1867 the cost of maintaining one prisoner for a year was $63.80. Today's cost is about $13,000 per man per year. Employee salaries account for much of that figure. There are 900 people working at San Quentin; 550 are uniformed guards.

Like most "correctional" facilities, San Quentin has its share of problems. Overcrowding is one; outbreaks of violence another. Drug abuse is a third.

San Quentin has an extensive rehabilitation program. But over a ten-year period, fifty percent of San Quentin's inmates will return to prison. Just how improvements in rehabilitation can be made in the face of increasing state and federal tax cuts concerns San Quentin's inmate and staff population.

Over the years, California politicians have often considered closing San Quentin. But finding places for three thousand men in an already overcrowded state prison system is a prob-

Richmond-San Rafael Bridge, from Point San Quentin

144

lem few want to tackle. A few Marinites might be relieved to have the grim monolith removed. But San Quentin's cold presence has not stopped real-estate developers from eyeing the peninsula. Prison or not, the peninsula's undeveloped hills near Larkspur Landing command unique bay views. Some say tract houses there will soon have Tiburon price tags. Transportation is excellent. Where the San Francisco and San Quentin ferry used to land, the Richmond–San Rafael Bridge now reaches across San Francisco Bay to Contra Costa County. The stage road to San Rafael is a six-lane highway. Less than a mile from the prison grounds, you can board a luxurious ferry, the Larkspur Ferry, for San Francisco. For convenient shopping nearby is Larkspur Landing, where rock was quarried only a few years ago.

San Rafael

The Franciscan fathers who founded Mission San Rafael Arcangel in 1817 would not have been surprised that Dr. W. W. DuBois, in the 1870s, recommended San Rafael to his medical colleagues as a good site for a convalescent home. What might have surprised the fathers was how long it took physicians to discover what they had known all along—San Rafael has a fine climate. The Franciscans had brought several hundred Coast Miwok Indians across the bay to live at the mission and recover from the respiratory and infectious diseases contracted in cold, foggy Yerba Buena.

There was another reason for building Mission San Rafael. Russian settlements on the California coast extended as far south as Mendocino County. The Spanish military at the presidio in Yerba Buena wanted to be sure the Russians did not come farther. So, while most of Marin fell under the mission's jurisdiction, buffer zones at Sausalito, Tiburon, and Point Reyes were held by the military.

In 1850, when San Rafael became the county seat, part of the mission, long since secularized and dismantled by the Mexican government, was used as the courthouse. When William T. Coleman arrived in 1871, San Rafael was a quiet dairy town with a population of fewer than two hundred. But the San Francisco commission merchant bought eleven hundred acres in the town, developed subdivisions, floated the Marin Water Company, built two hotels, helped underwrite the new court-

Fourth Street, San Rafael, circa 1910

Fourth Street newstand, San Rafael

HIGH SOCIETY

"Oh God, let me up into the paradise of San Francisco Society. Burlingame, Alta, Menlo Park, Atherton, Belvedere, San Rafael. . . ."

GERTRUDE ATHERTON
THE SISTERS-IN-LAW (1921)

THE DEVIL OF SAN RAFAEL

The Hookooeko of San Rafael say:

   Yu´-tenm´e-chah the Evil One lives in the hills just north of San Rafael; he travels about at night and sometimes comes and touches people when they are asleep, to frighten them.

BONNIE J. PETERSON (EDITOR)
DAWN OF THE WORLD: COAST MIWOK INDIANS (1976)

house, and sold a large tract of land in his eastern addition to the Sisters of Dominican College.

Other wealthy San Franciscans followed. So did schools, stables, and railroads. In 1906, after the earthquake, a tent city in San Rafael housed some two hundred homeless San Franciscans. One arrival was former lightweight boxer Billy Shannon. His training camp and bar, Shannon's Villa, on Fourth Street, became a popular gathering place for fighters and fans.

Another colorful enterprise arrived in 1911—the California Motion Picture Corporation. Taking pride in their authentic Western locations, the company managed to burn down a San Rafael office building while shooting a dramatic rescue scene. Recently, filmmaker George Lucas shot scenes for *American Graffiti* in the town. And from his San Rafael studios, he conceived the characters and special effects for *Star Wars*.

Today, San Rafael is still the county seat. Marin is governed by a five-member board of supervisors, elected by districts roughly equal in population (about 45,000 per district). One important supervisorial task is assisting unincorporated Marin communities with self-government. As one supervisor puts it, this is "close-up" work, which often involves helping to resolve internal community disputes as well as serving as community liaison with county, state, and federal agencies.

With a population of 45,000, San Rafael is Marin's largest town and its most urban. On its wide streets are some of Marin's highest office buildings and oldest storefronts. The town attracts teenagers roaring through in hopped-up "lowriders" and Sunday tourists sedately exploring the historic mission site and colorful Victorians. The downtown has suffered from competition with shopping malls on its suburban perimeter, but many of its unique stores remain. Who can fault a city with the cheapest copy center, finest French restaurant, oldest bank, and best newsstand in the county?

Point San Pedro

Point San Pedro's stubby thumb pokes into San Francisco Bay as if reaching to touch the slender finger of Point San Pablo in Contra Costa County. Like an hourglass, the bay waters narrow here where the fingers flirt, then open into San Pablo Bay.

San Rafael subdivisions line the southern shores of the point, but most of the northern shore is still undeveloped.

A VIEW OF SAN PABLO BAY

They stood out through the straits between Point Tiburon and the Isle of the Angels, where the tide ran fast. Then, for the first time, was Rezánov able to form a definite idea of the size and shape of this great natural harbor. To the south it extended beyond the peninsula in an unbroken sheet for some forty English miles. Ten miles to the north there was a gateway between the lower hills which Luis had alluded to as leading into the bay of Saint Pablo, another large body of tide-water, but inferior in depth and beauty to the Bay of San Francisco.

GERTRUDE ATHERTON
REZÁNOV (1906)

THE JOSS HOUSE

China Camp also had its Joss House where much incense was burned. The fisherman's "joss" or idol was consulted many times throughout the season. Each shrimper paid $2.50 a month to worship at the Joss House. English and Chin-chin instruction were offered at the San Pedro school by a Caucasian teacher for two dollars a month. History fails to record whether the fishermen took advantages of this education.

GEORGE PARRISH
"THE DEATH OF CHINA CAMP"
SAN FRANCISCO MAGAZINE
OCTOBER 1962

McNear's Beach is a county park, China Camp is a state park. The tract homes of Santa Venetia are part of unincorporated San Rafael.

McNears Beach

The name McNear is almost synonymous with Point San Pedro. Purchasing their first parcel here in 1869, the family owned 2,500 acres of the point by 1880. John McNear was president of the Petaluma–Santa Rosa Railroad. He also ran a steamer on Petaluma Creek and started a brickworks at San Pedro.

The McNear family resort on the point was a popular dancing spot and boating place for San Rafael residents in the 1930s. After two unsuccessful attempts to sell their beachside holdings in the 1950s and '60s, the family sold twenty-four acres of shorefront to the county in 1970. Today the park is well used; the swimming pool, picnic tables, and sandy beach attract thousands of summer visitors. Although the McNear family provided some colorful moments in Marin County history, none were quite as remarkable as the activities of their tenants just down the road at China Camp.

China Camp

One rickety pier stretches into the shallow cove at China Camp. On the pebble beach, just south of Rat Rock, a few worn buildings huddle under their tin roofs like derelicts snoozing under yesterday's newspapers. "Fresh Up with 7-Up" reads a faded sign on the side of the white clapboard coffee shop by the old boathouse. Six motorcycles are parked on the dirt road. Their owners drink beer on the beach and listen to "old Howie" strum "Somebody Stole My Gal" on his steel guitar.

"Pick it out, you old buzzard," laughs a man eating a pound of fresh bay shrimp at a picnic table.

A lone fishing boat putts slowly up to the pier. Frank Quan squats down to untangle a shrimp net. He is the last Chinese-American still living at China Camp. "I'm the only one here now," he says. "My brother has left and my cousin lives in San Rafael. My mother died eight years ago."

In 1865, thousands of Cantonese began arriving in the Bay Area. They were hired to build the transcontinental railroad

IMMIGRATION

**I thoroughly hate the barbarians because they
do not respect justice.
They continually promulgate harsh laws to
show off their prowess.
They oppress the overseas Chinese and also
violate treaties.
They examine for hookworms and practice
hundreds of despotic acts.**

INSCRIPTION FROM A WALL AT ANGEL ISLAND
IMMIGRATION STATION
ISLAND: POETRY AND HISTORY OF CHINESE
IMMIGRANTS ON ANGEL ISLAND 1910–1940
HIM MARK LAI, GENNY LIM, JUDY YUNG (1980)

China Camp

across the High Sierra. Many of the immigrants had no documents or working papers; in the night, transport vessels slipped past the immigration station on Alcatraz Island and deposited their passengers in a tiny cove on San Pablo Bay. That cove was China Camp.

After the railroad was completed in 1869, many Chinese returned to Marin to build the North Pacific Coast Railroad. Fifteen hundred Chinese lived in China Camp, which was one of twenty-six Chinese fishing villages on San Francisco Bay. The bay waters were rich with shrimp. At high tide, fishermen in lug-sailed junks picked the shrimp from nets fixed to stakes in the shallow water. The shrimp were dried on the hillsides, threshed by foot, and shipped to San Francisco. The hulls were sent to China, where they were used as fertilizer.

In the 1870s and '80s, economic recession hit San Francisco. A drought brought penniless farmers into the city, and the closing of the Comstock Lode brought miners. The newly unemployed found that many factory and mill jobs were taken by Chinese working at low wages. "Anti-coolie" clubs formed to lobby for the 1882 Exclusion Act. Caucasian gangs terrorized the Chinese, who were confined to seven blocks of Chinatown. Ten thousand Chinese fled to Marin County; three thousand came to China Camp. They built makeshift huts along the bay. The slopes behind the beach served as vegetable gardens. Landlord Erskine McNear charged one dollar in rent per person every month. Once again, shrimping was the livelihood. Thirty to forty tons a week were shipped to San Francisco by Captain Richard Bullis. Chinese were not allowed to trade on San Francisco docks.

In 1910, California fishing laws prohibited the use of fixed nets in the bay. Many China Camp residents left to look for jobs elsewhere in the county, although anti-Chinese sentiment still ran high in Marin. A fire in 1913 destroyed most of the old encampment.

In 1924 one man, a grocer at McNear's quarry, returned to China Camp. Quan Hock Quock developed a cone-shaped drag net that was legal and effective. He shrimped the bay until the 1950s, when mud began to destroy the shrimp beds. Frank Quan is Quan Hock's son. Frank is the third generation of his family to live here. Today he runs a boat-rental service and the coffee shop, which he leases from the state park. On weekends

County fair, Civic Center

JOHN LUND

**IN THE SHADOW OF "BIG PINK"—
PERFORMERS AND LECTURERS
AT MARIN CENTER**

Lillian Hellman, Count Basie, Gore Vidal,
Benny Goodman, William F. Buckley,
Pauline Kael, Ella Fitzgerald, Buckminster
Fuller, Joan Didion, San Francisco Ballet

149

he greets old-timers who've been coming to China Camp to fish for years. But he doesn't talk much about the old days.

For now, the park rangers have more to say about China Camp than Frank does. Park officials hope to restore some of the remaining buildings. Then perhaps the buildings themselves will tell the bleak story of the Chinese in Marin.

Santa Venetia

If Mabry McMahon had succeeded in 1914, Marin County would have "another Venice" on the South Fork of Gallinas Creek. But canals, palazzi, a railroad, and a ferry were projects more ambitious than a country soon to be preoccupied in Europe was ready to support. McMahon's plan fizzled.

Today, Santa Venetia does have a creekside subdivision. But, more pleasing to dreamers like McMahon, Santa Venetia has Marin County Civic Center, designed by Frank Lloyd Wright and completed after his death. The "Big Pink" took thirteen years to build and cost taxpayers more than they like to remember. On sixty acres of Point San Pedro, the deco-style Civic Center houses the county's administrative offices, law courts, main library; nearby is a community theater.

On August 7, 1970, Superior Court Judge Harold Haley was taken hostage in his Civic Center courtroom and killed by a seventeen-year-old black militant. Afterward, the county placed a bulletproof shield in the courtroom used for "sensitive" trials. Guards were posted in the halls. Side entrances to the mammoth Civic Center were closed. Today, you won't find many guards or even someone to help you find your way. State tax cuts have reduced many county administrative staffs to a skeleton. Some employees, under fire from taxpayers and overworked because of layoffs, are suffering from low morale. A few will tell you frankly they'll leave county government—and the Big Pink—as soon as they can find a job elsewhere.

Novato

Novato is Marin's last frontier. It's one of the county's newest cities and its fastest growing. Most of its eight shopping centers and ninety-odd subdivisions have appeared since 1960. You may have a hard time finding the "downtown," but you can't miss the real-estate offices. Greater Novato covers sev-

ON FOOT IN NOVATO

One farm has remained intact—the main truckers' road and crosstown highway goes right in front (close to downtown) of their still-operating farm. Walking north one can see groups of geese, guernsey cows, chickens, further even, by the condos that border their southern edge and of course obnoxious little dogs barking as you go by—on foot, that is.

RICHARD MEYERS
JOURNAL ENTRY
FEBRUARY 1980

REAL ESTATE BLUES

Then there is the real estate broker I talked to who had a client who was moving out to take a lifetime opportunity job with a San Francisco food company. He is moving from rural Virginia, where he has a charming three-bedroom Georgian house on three acres with a stable for his two horses.... The broker says the couple is "in shock." To get what he wants in Marin County he'd have to own the company he's going to work for.

ANTHONY COOK
"CALIFORNIA'S SOARING HOUSE PRICES"
NEW WEST
JUNE 6, 1977

Bel Marin Keys, Novato

enty square miles and includes the unincorporated communities of Black Point, Bel Marin Keys, and Loma Verde. The "city" covers twenty-three square miles and includes the historic community of Ignacio, just south of Novato.

Growth has been Novato's blessing and its curse. Real estate in Novato is still within the means of Bay Area residents who could not afford to live anywhere else in Marin. A secretary may find an affordable apartment here, and a family of six may find a house. One hundred and twenty-two members of the 620-person San Francisco Police Force live in Novato. So do many former U.S. Air Force personnel who settled here after their tours of duty at Hamilton Air Force Base.

But Novato developed quickly, without careful planning; its public services are overburdened, its social problems serious. "One of the problems of rapid growth," says Fifth District Supervisor Gail Wilhelm, "is a large influx of people who don't identify with the community. The social fabric is disrupted. We have an unusual kind of crime in Novato. Gangs of young adults between the ages of nineteen and twenty-four who are destructive to property."

A far cry from the days when Fernando Feliz grazed longhorns on the ridges of Rancho Novato. By 1856, most of Rancho Novato belonged to Joseph Sweetser and Francis C. Delong, two businessmen who planted 20,000 apple, 3,600 pear, and 2,000 apricot trees along Novato Creek. "The world's largest orchard" pleased the palates of fruit-hungry Californians, as well as New Yorkers, Britons, and Australians.

Novato's "old town" grew along Novato Creek, but the rail depot was the focus of "new town," now called "old town," through which the San Rafael–Petaluma train passed three times a day. In 1914 the town was about as Western as a place can get. Grant Avenue had wooden sidewalks and horse troughs. Cowboys herded cattle through the streets. Truck gardeners peddled fresh vegetables on the roadsides. Small dairies provided butter and cheese for San Francisco.

The Depression ruined Novato's orchard and poultry businesses. Postwar speculators bought abandoned farmland, and in the late fifties, developers moved in. One historic site spared from surveyors and bulldozers was Olompali, three and

NOVATO HAD WORLD'S LARGEST ORCHARD IN LATE 1860s

By the late 1860s, when Black Point was a rugged wilderness favored by elk hunters and Rancho San Jose was mostly grazing land, Rancho de Novato was considered the largest orchard in the world! As well as meeting U. S. demands, DeLong and Sweetser shipped apples to Australia. Apples were sorted for the San Francisco winter market in a building which held 20,000 boxes of apples at one time. Poorer grades of apples were turned into cider and vinegar. The partners had 20 vinegar vats, each with a 2800-gallon capacity.

MARIN COUNTY
HISTORICAL SOCIETY BULLETIN
JUNE 1975

Condominiums, Novato

a half miles north of Novato on Highway 101. Rancho Olompali, soon to become a state park, was the only Marin grant awarded a Native American Indian. Although Chief Camillo Ynitia sold most of his nine-thousand-acre ranch shortly before his death in 1856, part of his adobe still stands.

Herbert Rowland is the great-grandson of Ignacio Pacheco, who received Rancho San Jose, in Ignacio just south of Novato, in 1849. With six partners, Rowland owns Pacheco Ranch Winery, the only commercial winery in Marin County.

"It's always been a special kind of thing to have a Marin County wine," says Rowland's brother-in-law, Jamie Meves. "We will continue to make wines that are solely from Marin County grapes."

Just across the road from the Pacheco family ranch and clapboard farmhouse is another unusual operation, on land once part of Rancho San Jose. It's Hamilton Air Force Base. The two-thousand-acre facility has been the focus of a heated countywide debate. How will the mothballed base, once an Aerospace Defense Command, be used? Pro-aviationists favor building a commercial airport here, with feeder flights to major Bay Area airports. Others would like to see residential development at Hamilton, perhaps even Solar Village, endorsed by former State Architect Sym van der Ryn. Arguing that better aviation facilities are more important to the county than model housing, San Francisco's airport director recently complained, "Marin County can stick its head in the sand for only so long." Many believe the real issue is whether Marin County residents will have the final say in how the land is used. Responding to the Port of Oakland's bid for commercial aviation at Hamilton, one county supervisor replied, "There's going to be a full-scale war before we allow the Port of Oakland to occupy land in Marin, whether they want to operate an airport or a pizza parlor."

Black Point

Black Point crouches by the Petaluma River just before it empties into San Pablo Bay. Grandview was the name developer Rudolph Danmeyer used to lure San Francisco bass fishermen to his tiny Black Point lot sites. Some of his lots were offered as a bonus to purchasers of *Collier's Encyclopedia*. Many of the vacation cabins still remain. Hay barges no longer

THE FUTURE OF MARIN

I think Marin is going to grow as a magnet. If one of our huge problems of this decade is energy, then Phoenix certainly loses its attraction because it's fully air-conditioned. There's going to be more population flight from the colder places, too, like the Northeast and Chicago. Marin is ideal; you neither have to heat nor cool in a big way. Also, if we're going to have big social problems in adjusting to the new realities of life, then safety or security is going to be uppermost in a lot of affluent people's minds. This community has a very good record for safety and security. . . . I think that you are going to have an increasing influx of affluent people. Whether this area can accommodate them or wants to accommodate them is another thing. For all these reasons I think housing is going to become enormously expensive. People are going to put a lot more money into their home, having purchased it already at some ridiculous price.

PAUL ERDMAN
"MARIN IN THE 80S"
INTERVIEW BY STEVE MCNAMARA
PACIFIC SUN
JANUARY 25–31, 1980

Petaluma River, Black Point

stop at Black Point Landing, but there's a popular boat launch now, and many new homes have been built in the area. Black Forest, on the western side of town, attracts thousands of weekend visitors in the months of August and September.

In the dappled, oak-covered hills of Black Forest, three thousand craftspeople, actors, cooks, musicians, and puppeteers, fully outfitted in Elizabethan costume, stage the Renaissance Pleasure Faire. Coproduced by the Living History Center, the Faire is a re-creation of an Elizabethan market and fair day.

Half-timbered stalls and colorful tents line the dirt paths of Black Forest. Fishmongers, balladeers, and tonsured monks with overflowing flagons stroll the grounds, speaking in Elizabethan English. "Huzzah, wilst buy a churro?" calls a baker from her shop. The washerwomen at the water pump gossip loudly. Insults fly first, then laundry, then fists.

"Make way for the Queen," calls a barrel-chested courtier. In a canopied sedan chair, Queen Bess is paraded through the crowds. Jugglers, merchants, and mummers pause to bow. At the Ben Jonson Theatre, the Queen addresses the fairgoers seated on hay bales. A jig, a song, and a bawdy comedy follow.

"Market days were much more fun than going to the supermarket is now," says Phyllis Patterson, who created the first Faire in 1963. "It's a microcosm of many lifestyles."

Marin County supplies many of the "lifestyles" and people willing to participate in the unique event. The county gets a lot in return. "Begone, dull care," say the thousands of Marinites who visit Elizabethan England every summer, " 'tis time for the Faire."

Boat landing, Petaluma River

Renaissance Pleasure Faire, Black Point

Detail, Mission San Rafael Arcangel

SAN RAFAEL

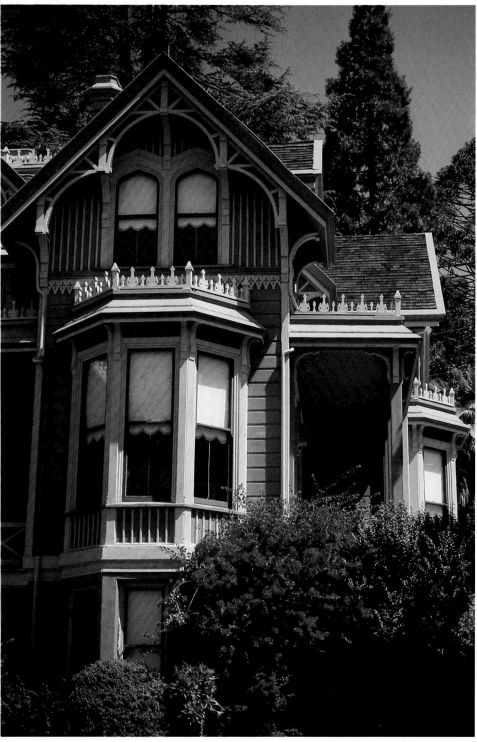

Marin County Historical Society, Boyd Park

Fourth Street Clock, San Rafael

Mission San Rafael Arcangel

Guide Dogs for the Blind, San Rafael

JOHN LUND

Waterfront sign, San Rafael

Dominican College, San Rafael

Saint Vincent's School, San Rafael

Coffee shop, Fourth Street, San Rafael

SANTA VENETIA

Marin County Civic Center

Rooftop garden, Marin County Civic Center

CHINA CAMP

Fishing pier

Novato City Hall

Billiard parlor, Grant Avenue

Stafford Lake Park, Indian Valley Road

Novato

Hillside home, Novato

BLACK POINT

Cabins near Petaluma River

The Song Mt. Tamalpais Sings

This is the last place. There is nowhere else to go.
    Human movements,
        but for a few,
    are Westerly.
    Man follows the Sun.

This is the last place. There is nowhere else to go.
    Or follows what he thinks to be the
    movement of the Sun
    It is hard to feel it, as a rider,
    on a spinning ball.

This is the last place. There is nowhere else to go.
    Centuries and hordes of us,
    from every quarter of the earth,
    now piling up,
    and each wave going back
    to get some more.

This is the last place. There is nowhere else to go.
    "My face is the map of the Steppes,"
    she said, on this mountain, looking West.

    My blood set singing by it,
    to the old tunes,
    Irish, still,
    among these Oaks.

This is the last place. There is nowhere else to go.
  This is why
  once again we celebrate
  the great Spring Tides.

  Beaches are strewn again with Jasper,
  Agate, and Jade.
  The Mussel-rock stands clear.

This is the last place. There is nowhere else to go.
  This is why
  once again we celebrate the
  Headland's huge, cairn-studded, fall
  into the Sea.

This is the last place. There is nowhere else to go.
  For we have walked the jeweled beaches
  at the feet of the final cliffs
  of all Man's wanderings.

This is the last place.
There is nowhere else we need to go.

       —LEW WELCH
       (1926–1971)

Acknowledgements

Jack Mason

Louise Teather

Two Marin writers—Jack Mason and Louise Teather—contributed enormously to the writing of *Marin: The Place, the People.*

Jack Mason is the author of seven books on Marin County: *Ben's Auto Stage* (1967); *Point Reyes: The Solemn Land* (1970); *Early Marin,* with Helen Van Cleave Park (1971); *Last Stage for Bolinas,* with Thomas Barfield (1973); *Summer Town* (1974); *The Making of Marin 1850–1975,* with Helen Van Cleave Park (1975); *Earthquake Bay* (1976). All are published by North Shore Books, Inverness, California. Mr. Mason's carefully researched, colorful histories, as well as his quarterly periodical, the *Point Reyes Historian,* have been invaluable resources, providing much of the historical background presented in *Marin: The Place, the People.* We are also grateful to Mr. Mason for reading and commenting on the manuscript.

Louise Teather has lived in Tiburon since 1946. Her articles on Marin history, and her book, *Discovering Marin* (Fairfax, CA: The Tamal Land Press, 1974) helped us identify many places of historical interest in Marin County. Mrs. Teather generously shared her personal files on Marin County and read *Marin: The Place, the People* in manuscript and galley stages.

We also wish to thank many other people who gave their time and energy to the writing and production of *Marin: The Place, the People.* We are particularly grateful to: William Abrahams, our editor, who guided us through what at times seemed a hopelessly complex and difficult project; Abigail Hemstreet, who edited many drafts of the manuscript and offered her often needed encouragement to the writer; Elna Conover, whose many contributions included filing and cataloguing numerous transparencies; John Lund, who provided additional photography; Richard Meyers, whose research assistance was especially valuable in preparing the "marginalia"; Catherine Hopkins, who first suggested we collaborate on a "Marin County book"; Sharon Cooke, who typed two drafts of the manuscript; Karen Gillis, who coordinated production for Holt, Rinehart and Winston; Trent Duffy, who supervised copy-editing for Holt; Tarja Beck, who assisted in mechanical production; and Fred Hill, our agent.

Our thanks also go to: Elsie Mazzini of the Marin County Historical Society; Ruth Costello of the Society for Comparative Philosophy; Mary Ann Shaffer and Dick Shaffer; John and Jean Burroughs; Phil and Susan Frank; Steve Obrebski; Rita Abrams; Bill Alexander; Margaret Azevedo; Marjorie Macris; Jim Van de Weg; Phyllis Miller; Jim Kidder; T.J. Nelson; Patrick Vaughn; Debby Dohm; and Russell Keil. And finally, we thank all the people whose interviews were used in the text of *Marin: The Place, the People.*

Jane Futcher
Robert Conover

GRAPHIC CREDITS

Typography
Turner, Brown & Yeoman, Inc.,
San Francisco, California

Color Separations
Offset Separations Corporation,
Turin, Italy

Offset Lithography
Pearl, Pressman, Liberty Printers,
Philadelphia, Pennsylvania

Paper
Warren's Lustro Enamel Dull from
Alling and Cory, New York,
New York

Binding
A. Horowitz and Sons,
Fairfield, New Jersey

Index

JOHN LUND